MW01294259

Living Under The Cross

by
Bear Clifton

Cover Photography: The cross atop Garcia Trail
Azusa, CA
Photo by Gus Cruz

What Others Are Saying...

"Bear's humorous and honest writing has a way of disarming you, then touching your soul."

"Filled with wisdom and why-didn't-I-think-of-that moments."

"This book is absolutely needed for our toxic times."

"A treasure-trove of insights."

"I appreciate the meaningful way he unpacks specific Bible texts. Bear can say more in 2-pages than I've heard in many a sermon."

"Like 'Train Yourself To Be Godly', this book is powerful to use one-on-one but also works great in small groups or classes."

"Not a book to read only once. I'll be referring back to this one often."

Devotional Index

Introduction 5
"Blessed are the poor in spirit, for theirs is the kingdom of heaven."
    The Right View of God 10
    The Right View Of Ourselves 13
    The Right View Of Lost People 16
    The Right View Of Evangelism 19
    The Right View Of Holiness 22
"Blessed are those who mourn, for they shall be comforted."
    Life Change Begins Here 26
    Life Change Requires Suffering 29
    Life Change Requires Repentance 32
    Life Change Can Happen For You 35
"Blessed are the meek, for they shall inherit the earth."
    Judge Not Knottiness 39
    When Judging Is The Right Thing To Do 42
    A Case Study In Judgmentalism 45
    Two Ways To Know If You're Judgmental 48
    Two More Traits Of Judgmentalism 51
"Blessed are those who hunger and thirst for righteousness."
    Friendship With God Means Seeking Him 55
    Friendship With God Means Listening 58
    Friendship With God Means Knowing Him 61
    Friendship With God Means Pleasing Him 64
    Friendship With God: It Takes Time To Grow 67
"Blessed are the merciful, for they shall receive mercy."
    Love Your Enemies? Some Objections 71
    Love Your Enemies? Some Conditions 74
    Love Your Enemies: Bless Them, Don't Curse 77

Love Your Enemies: Forgiveness (What It's Not) 80
Love Your Enemies: Forgiveness (What It Is) 83
"Blessed are the pure in heart, for they shall see God."
The Cycle Of Sin: Desire 87
The Cycle Of Sin: Deception 90
The Cycle Of Sin: Disobedience 93
The Cycle Of Sin: Death 96
"Blessed are the peacemakers, for they shall be called sons of God."
Peacemaking: Why It's Important 100
Peacemaking: What It's Not 103
Peacemaking: Its Foundation 106
Brouhaha Training: Forbearance 109
Brouhaha Training: Dealing With Gray Areas 112
Brouhaha Training: To Arms! 115
"Blessed are those who are persecuted for righteousness' sake."
Sharing Our Faith: Be Incarnational 119
Sharing Our Faith: Be Inclusively Exclusive 122
Sharing Our Faith: Be Informed 125
"Rejoice and be glad for your reward is great in heaven."
Joy: The Birthright Of The Christian 129
Rejoice In The Goodness Of God 132
Rejoice IN The Lord 135
Rejoice WITH The Lord 138
Rejoice FOR The Lord 141

Introduction

"I have been crucified with Christ. It is no longer I who live, but Christ who lives in me." ~ Galatians 2:20

We live in a calloused age.

We've seen worse times, for sure. In fact, a case could be made that the last fifty years in America might possibly represent the finest half century any human society has ever experienced in terms of raw national peace, prosperity and technological advancement.

But you wouldn't know it if you took a careful look around.

We're angry. Name-calling and scorn spews from our politics. The college campus exists to fester outrage, not foster the intellect. Rather than attempt a civil conversation, we run into our social media bunkers, and lob our incendiary comments and tweets at each other.

We're divided. The nuclear family has blown up. Red state – blue state. The world of *Green Book* and *Hidden Figures* seems positively Bronze Age compared to now, yet race relations remain like a faultline ready to crack.

We're emotional trainwrecks. Physically we're great. I can find a dozen articles right now on *Flipboard* on how to do a proper plank. Meanwhile, addiction is laying waste to small-town America. Depression rates are reaching new heights across all age groups. Suicides are skyrocketing among white middle age males.

We're profane and cynical. Do you know what the greatest difference was between the 1976 *A Star Is Born* with the 2018 remake? Oh, about 300 F-bombs. But the new film got one thing right. We're *shalloooooow.*

We've kicked God to the curb. Twice in the last twenty years we came within a whisker of seeing everything fall apart on us – after 9/11 and then again after the 2008 housing meltdown. There was pain, to be sure, but our great-grandparents know how much worse it might have been. The center held. Yet it's odd how we've treated God since then. We've traded him in for mindfulness training. We've ripped up his sexual boundaries. We've put his people in our crosshairs. If the dogma lies deep in you, beware.

The times we live in are truly toxic. So is there anything that can serve as an antidote to this poison that our culture keeps serving up? Can anything pull us back from the abyss of despair and disintegration we keep flirting with?

Yes, there is. It's found in the title of this book. The world needs for the group of people who claim to be followers of Jesus Christ to begin *living under the Cross.*

Far from being just a piece of jewelry to put around your neck, or a nice tattoo for your arm, a cross is one of the most radical symbols ever created, pointing to one of the most radical lifestyles ever proposed.

Jesus expected his followers to observe a daily practice of *dying to themselves*, with the cross serving as a metaphor for that habit.

> *"Jesus said to them all, 'If anyone would come after me, let him deny himself and take up his cross daily and follow me." ~ Luke 9:23*

This is all nice poetry, but what would such a life look like at street-level? Jesus gave the answer on a Judean hillside when he stood up before a crowd of followers and gave one of history's most remarkable speeches, known today as the *Sermon On The Mount*, beginning with nine short sayings we now call the *Beatitudes.*

In the Beatitudes, Jesus describes what it looks like when we *die to ourselves.* Living under the Cross is marked by humility, and sorrow for my own brokenness, which leads to showing gentleness to others. (Imagine those virtues coming from the White House or Washington Post.)

It's a life that derives its strength from hungering after God, that consequently grows in mercy, and purity and peacemaking. It's a life that devotes itself to the promotion of good, no matter the cost, and results in joy, which not even persecution can stamp out.

This book is a collection of 42 short devotions – gathered under the headings of each of Jesus' nine Beatitudes (some count eight) – which attempt to wrestle with the implications of what Jesus is asking us when he tells us to *"take up our cross daily and follow him".*

What our culture desperately needs most from followers of Christ today is not that we be politically active (though there's nothing wrong with that.) It's not that we be culturally accommodating (there are all sorts of things wrong with that.) What culture needs from us (whether it admits it or not) is that we attempt to live the life our Lord called us to live.

I take back what I said a moment ago. Such a life is not a radical life. It is an *impossible* life. I can't live it, unless I take time to meditate over and over again on what Jesus did for me on that cross, then desperately cry out to him to live through me.

Bear Clifton

8

"Blessed are the poor in spirit, for theirs is the kingdom of heaven."

The Right View Of God

"For I have no pleasure in the death of anyone, declares the Lord God; so turn, and live." – Ezekiel 18:32

Life under the Cross requires that we make the attempt to look at things around us through the eyes of Jesus. In Luke 15, the religious leaders come and question Jesus about why he hangs out with sinful people. In response, he tells them three stories in succession: about a lost coin, a lost sheep, and a lost son (do you detect a theme?)

The Prodigal Son story is particularly rich because it's a veritable 3-act play with a sweeping cast of players. Each character has something to teach us about Jesus' perspective. So from the description of the father in the story we learn how Jesus viewed God his Father.

People like the Pharisees – the legalists – tend to see God, not like a father but like a Godfather – a trigger-happy deity who loves nothing more than to jump on people for blowing it. Picture God as Marlon Brando saying, "See dese ten commandments here? Ya mess around with dem, it's coitains for ya pal, capiche? I'll rub ya right out."

But then there were the Sadducees – the libertines – who liked to talk about how God is love (pronounced *luvvv*) and because he is *luvvv*, he's nothing but supportive of you living however you wish....no questions asked.

Both are mistaken and out of balance.

The Bible says that God is love. But it's a robust love, expressed through both holiness and mercy. The father allows the son to break fellowship with him and leave. He doesn't beg him to reconsider or change his rules to suit the son. (God is holy.) But then when the son comes to his senses and returns, the father is first in line to welcome him home (God is merciful.)

God hates sin and what it's done to us and his good creation. One of the first tasks Jesus sets out to do in us is to start breaking us of our sin by giving us boundaries and disciplining us when we ignore them. He does this *because* he loves us. The libertines forget or minimize this. It's why the Sadducees were sad, you see.

But God as a good, good father (*"It's who you are..."*) doesn't want to lose any of us. He longs to give us mercy. *"Mercy triumphs over judgment,"* James said (2:13). The legalists forget or minimize this. They actually believe that *judgment* triumphs over mercy. (And seem to get a real charge out of it.)

It's worth considering that both the legalists (the Pharisees) and the libertines (the Sadducees) found Jesus' ideas of spirituality to be a threat, and signed off on his execution.

But don't you go trying to put God in a box. Or he'll rub ya right out, *capiche?*

1. It's tough to keep balanced spiritually. Is there one side or the other that you drift toward when you're not careful - legalist (Pharisee) or libertine (Sadducee)?

2. Explain what the phrase "Mercy triumphs over judgment" means to you in one or two sentences.

12

Prayer

Father God, forgive me for the times when I've tried to put you in a box. Help me not to forget the truth that because you are love, you are both holy and merciful. And let me not forget in my dealings with others, that if push comes to shove, mercy is to triumph over judgment.

The Right View Of Ourselves

"You, when you have done everything you were told to do, should say, 'We are unworthy servants; we have only done our duty.'" – Luke 17:10

If we want to learn to see through Jesus' eyes, a great tutorial to use is the story of the Prodigal Son. Here we learn the right way to view *ourselves*.

Religious people must continually be on guard against an attitude of spiritual pride, which crops up when we begin thinking, "I'm on God's side. There must be something about me that's better than other people."

The older brother in the story, who stayed on the farm and helped his father, probably said to himself more than once, "Hey, I didn't demand to have my share of the inheritance. I resisted the urge to get happy feet. I'm not the one who acted like an idiot. Aren't I something?"

We know that the Pharisees thought this way. In Luke 18-9-14 Jesus quotes a Pharisee who runs into a tax collector, then prays, *"God I thank you that I am not like other men, unjust, adulterers, or even like this tax collector."* Such ugliness on parade.

Yet this spirit can seep into our heart so easily. You can be walking downtown and see a man in old, tattered clothes rummaging through a trash barrel for soda cans, and rather than feel compassion for him, you feel condescension, even offense. *Why couldn't he have made good choices like I did? God, I thank you that I am not like other men. God, aren't you lucky to have someone like me on your side?*

But we must never go there in our thinking. Why? Because *it's a lie!* It's simply not true that you're better than other people. The doctrine of sin overrules you. The cross overrules you. You needed Christ to die for you there just like every other human on the planet.

In 1 Corinthians 15:10 Paul writes, *"By the grace of God I am what I am."* That's a good verse to keep telling yourself.

Grace – God's undeserved kindness – enfolds us in so many ways we seldom appreciate. You didn't have a choice of who your parents were. Or what country you were born in. Or what century you were born in. Or what kind of health you'd be given. Or what kind of wealth you'd have access to. These are all aspects of things you had no control over. Of *grace.*

If you're stronger than another person, you should say, *"By the grace of God I am what I am,"* even though you might exercise every day (and you should.) If you're smart, a veritable Rhodes scholar, you should say, *"By the grace of God I am what I am,"* even though you might study hard every day (and you should.) And if you're a Christian, you've repented of your sins, and accepted Christ, you should say, *"By the grace of God, I am what I am,"* even though in a manner of speaking, you had the good sense to respond.

1. Why do you think spiritual pride is such an easy attitude to let slip into our hearts?

2. How might repeating the phrase, "By the grace of God I am what I am" several times each day help me?

Prayer

Lord Jesus, forgive me for the times when I allow spiritual pride to distort the way I see myself and others. Thank you that you died for me on the cross. If you hadn't done that, I would have been lost forever. Help me to never forget that 'by the grace of God, I am what I am'.

The Right View Of Lost People

"Now the tax collectors and sinners were all drawing near to hear him. And the Pharisees and scribes grumbled, saying, 'This man receives sinners and eats with them.' " – Luke 15:1-2

How do you look at the people in your life who don't share your faith, go to church or have many, if any, God-thoughts?

When you live under the Cross, there is only one way to see them, which Jesus explains in the story of the Prodigal Son. The religious leaders of Jesus' day were offended by his ease at hobnobbing with those they labeled "sinners". They're like the Elder Brother in the story who reveals later in the story that he despises his prodigal brother for the choices he has made.

The Pharisees no doubt believed they were on the side of the angels to disdain those who were lost. Were these people not living, breathing spiritual contaminants? They could weaken your faith. They did repugnant things. They're ripe for judgment. They're morally foolish. They get what they deserve. To hang with them must mean you approve of them, or secretly want to be like them.

But Jesus – in intentionally being a *friend of sinners* – modeled what has now become a trite – but seldom practiced – cliché. He could love the sinner while hating their sin.

The older son in the parable, like the Pharisees, couldn't do this. He hated this brother for what he had done. He wouldn't even call him his brother. When his father throws a party for his brother after his return, he says to his father, *"But when this **son of yours** came, who has devoured your property with prostitutes, you killed the fattened calf for him!"* Notice his words and the spit in his voice: *this son of yours.*

But the father then reminds him not to see the sin, but to see a brother restored, saved from sin. The father says, *"It was fitting to celebrate and be glad, for this **your brother** was dead, and is alive; he was lost, and is found."* Again pay attention. This is *your brother.*

Paul says, *"One has died for all...Therefore we regard no one according to the flesh"* (2 Cor.5:14,16). Jesus' death for you and me on the cross must change the way we look at others.

Somehow we must learn to look at lost people as potential, future members of our family. Just the mere fact that we call them "lost" suggests that they need to be found. Do you have the faith to see that foul-mouthed coworker down at the shop as someone who one day might be sitting beside you in church singing praise to God? Do you have the faith to see that rebellious daughter of yours who's shacking up with her third boyfriend in as many years, forgiven, pure, and happily married?

1. How many close relationships do you have with those who aren't followers of Christ? Write down two or three specific things you can do to be a 'friend of sinners'.

2. C.S. Lewis wrote *"It is a serious thing to live in a society of possible gods and goddesses, to remember that the dullest most uninteresting person you can talk to may one day be a creature which, if you saw it now, you would be strongly tempted to worship, or else a horror and a corruption such as you now meet, if at all, only in a nightmare. All day long we are, in some degree helping each other to one or the other of these destinations."*
What do you think Lewis means here?

Prayer

Spirit of God, change my heart, and help me to see the lost people in my life the way Jesus modeled. Touch my imagination and help me to creatively find ways to spend more time and conversation with the unchurched people you've placed in the orbit of my life.

The Right View Of Evangelism

"For the Son of Man came to seek and to save the lost." – Luke 19:10

Once you begin to understand that God wants no one to perish but everyone to come to repentance, and once you begin to look at yourself as being what you are by the grace of God, and once you begin to look at the lost as future family members who need to be set free from the poison of their sin, *then* you will start to view evangelism rightly.

A recent Barna study showed that nearly half of Millennial Christians think that evangelism is wrong. Older Christians shouldn't be swift to say *tsk-tsk.* Truth be told, a lot of Christians look at evangelism as the worst thing that Jesus has asked them to do.

There's a great old hymn called, *I Love To Tell The Story,* but I think most Christians who sing that song are lying through their teeth. If they were to sing the song honestly, it would be titled, *I Kinda, Sorta Like To Tell The Story.*

But the apostle Paul said in Romans 1:16, *"I am not ashamed of the gospel, for it is the power of God for salvation to everyone who believes."*

Evangelism seen rightly shouldn't be a bother. It's introducing people to your best friend, the most important being in the universe, and the one who can bring forgiveness, freedom, hope and purpose to your life. If you were buds with the actor Chris Pratt, and he came to school or work one day to meet you during lunch, would you be embarrassed to introduce him to your friends? (Besides, Chris Pratt is not afraid to tell others about his faith. Google it.)

Not only should evangelism become natural and real to us, but it should become a priority as well. In the parable of the lost sheep, Jesus says of the shepherd, *"Does he not leave the 99 in the open country, and go after the one that is lost until he finds it?"* In the parable of the lost coin, he says of the woman, *"Does she not light a lamp and sweep the house and seek diligently until she finds it?"* Notice the words: Go after, sweep the house, seek diligently, leave no dust-bunny unturned.

I heard a pastor once pray a long prayer in his church, asking God to bring in the lost through the doors of the church from the north and south and east and west. But I thought as he was praying, "No Lord, that's wrong. We need to be asking the Lord to give us courage to go to them."

Jesus said, "Follow me, and I will make you fishers of men." Anyone who loves to fish knows that the fish don't come to you; you have to go to them. And one other thing: You have to catch fish before you can clean them. If you insist that a fish not be smelly, slimey and gross before you bring it into your boat, you'll never catch a thing. So why do so many Christians turn their nose up when a shattered, lost soul comes in to the church looking for help?

1. Do you *love* to tell the story? Explain your answer.

2. Circle any of the following things you ought to do to get better at fishing for souls.
Pray More * Learn Reasons For My Faith * Receive evangelism training * Figure out natural ways to insert Jesus into my conversations * Practice * Give up that big sin I'm not giving up * Stop being so busy * Fall in love with Jesus more * Open my mouth

Prayer

Lord, you promised to make me a fisher of men and women. So I ask you to fulfill this promise in me. I don't want to get to heaven and realize I had all these opportunities for helping others get closer to you, and missed them.

The Right View Of Holiness

"For this is the love of God, that we keep his commandments. And his commandments are not burdensome." – 1 John 5:3

Living under the Cross will also change the way we look at holiness, a lesson illustrated by the older brother in the story of the Prodigal Son.

When the prodigal son returns, and his father kills the fatted calf for him, the older brother is incensed and refuses to go in to the party. He says to his father *"Look, these many years I have served you."* (The NIV says, "I have *slaved* for you.") *"And I never disobeyed your command, yet you never gave me a young goat, that I might celebrate with my friends."* (Luke 15:29)

His very words show that the way he thinks of holiness is defective. Here he's been obeying his father, and how does he look at it? *My brother's out having fun while I'm back here **slaving** for you.* How many times have we thought: *Oh I'm a Christian now. No more fun for me.* It's the Mardi Gras fallacy. *Let's party it up while we can, 'cuz the next 40 days are going to be a drudgery.*

Could we think this through logically for a moment? Who is going to end up happier in life – someone who goes around carousing each weekend, staggers into the house at 3 AM, wakes up puking, can't think straight, can barely hold a job, can scarcely hold his marriage together, hardly knows his kids – or someone who doesn't do all those things?

Who's going to look in the mirror at the end of his or her life and feel better? Sure there's pleasure in sin. The Bible says as much. I'm sure at first, the younger son was having the time of his life when he ran away. But it's a pleasure that never lasts. And this movie always ends the same way. Addiction. Poverty. Regret. Shame.

Where is true happiness found? It's found in *obeying God*. In keeping his commandments. King David wrote in Psalm 16, *"In your presence there is fullness of joy, at your right hand are pleasures forevermore."* There's nothing to be gained or learned by ever giving in to sin.

The older son griped because his dad never gave them a goat to celebrate with. But whose fault was that? Did the father ever forbid it? No! In fact, the father turns around and says, *"Son, you are always with me, and all that is mine is yours."*

Christian, do you know that you're home right now? You just need to click your heels together three times and you'll be there. And if your life of faith has seemed droll and drab lately, whose fault is that? You need to look at your life the way this parable tells you to look at your life. You are always with the Father. You are forgiven of everything you have ever done wrong. You are an heir of eternal life. And the Holy Spirit is inside of you to teach you and help you live rightly.

You're not missing out on any true joy by being a Christian. And you should never envy those who are adrift in their sin. It will all dry up on them in the end. And then it will enslave them, and destroy them.

Don't envy them. Instead pity them. Love them. Pray for them. Go to them and share with them the hope that is in you. Introduce them to Real Joy.

1. Why do you think the "pleasures forevermore" that God gives sometimes seem less desirable than the pleasures our sin offers?

2. What would you tell the older brother if he came and asked you for advice?

Prayer

Father, you are always with me, and everything you have is mine in Christ. Jesus you said that if I loved you, I would obey you. So Spirit of God, would you increase my love for you. Fill me to overflowing, that I would see the pleasures of sin as they really are – lifeless and empty.

"Blessed are those who mourn, for they will be comforted."

Life Change Begins Here

"Come, eat of my bread, and drink of the wine I have mixed. Leave your simple ways, and live, and walk in the way of insight." – Proverbs 9:5-6

Christianity specializes in changing lives for the better. You come to Christ when you are one thing. As you follow Christ, you become another thing.

I've discovered through years of reading the Bible that this moral journey is beautifully described over and over again, sometimes in the most obscure places. I recently read Proverbs 9:5-6 and laughed out loud, because here it was again – an invitation from God to open my broken, sinful heart to him, that he might bring something more loving and holy from it.

It begins with just the first word: *Come.*

The moral journey begins with you coming to Jesus. The healing of your soul and the rebuilding of your life cannot happen until you bow your knees to him. *"Come to me, all you who are weary and burdened, and I will give you rest,"* Jesus said (Matthew 11:28).

You don't say, *"I can't come to Jesus. I'm weary and burdened. He doesn't want a mess like me."* Such thinking is all wrong. It's precisely *because* you're weary and burdened that Jesus wants you to come. You don't clean up your act *and then* come to Jesus. He already knows you can't clean up your act. It's too late. It's why he died for you. So come as you are.

But then notice what the proverb says next. *Come, eat of my bread.* We then must be fed.

After inviting the weary and burdened to come to him, Jesus then says, *"Take my yoke upon you and **learn from me**, for I am gentle and humble in heart, and you will find rest for your souls."* (Matthew 11:29).

We've seen the tale of the moral journey in a thousand movies, where the weak or wounded or misguided or selfish main character comes into the presence of a guide or mentor who will train them, and release the hero inside of them. *The Matrix. Star Wars. The Mask of Zorro. The Karate Kid. A Christmas Carol.*

The greatest stories are all based in some fashion on the *Great Story* told in Scripture of Christ, who comes to earth from heaven to call us to our true destiny. But this journey is birthed in grace. It is not something we can obtain on our own. So we must *come* to the Lord and Master and present ourselves to him. And then we grant him permission to train us.

"Take my yoke upon you and learn from me."

A yoke is a heavy, wooden collar that binds two oxen together. Once you're yoked, you don't leave the other's side. Too many people come to Christ out of their need, then as soon as that need eases up, or this Christian-thing gets too demanding or too boring, they're gone. Or they mess up, then give up. They fail and bail.

No, my friend. That won't cut it. To take the moral journey from sin to Christlikeness will require us learning from Jesus. Learning is a process. It's hard work. We're not going to understand everything at first. Some things we're going to learn – especially about ourselves – will be very painful to hear. And difficult to leave behind.

The temptation to run will never be far away. This is why a yoke is necessary. But those who submit to this yoke, and accept the pain it will bring, are the ones who in the end will find true rest.

1. Why do many find it difficult to come to Christ?

2. Can you think of specific areas of your life where you would want Jesus to bring his healing and order? Based on the reading, how will that happen?

Prayer

Jesus, Bread of Life, feed me. You said that man does not live by bread alone but by every word that comes from the mouth of God. So may your word dwell in me richly. Teach me the discipline of a daily "quiet time" with you. Those who meditate on your word day and night will become like trees planted by streams of water. In time, may that be true of me, dear Lord.

Life Change Requires Suffering

"Come, eat of my bread and drink of the wine I have mixed. Leave your simple ways, and live, and walk in the way of insight." – Proverbs 9:5-6

This little proverb describes the journey of how a life can change for the better. First, we must come...come to Jesus, for we were made by God and for God, and without a relationship with him, we'll be lost before we even begin the journey. Then we must "eat of his bread". We must let Jesus teach us and train us how to live rightly.

The phrase *"and drink of the wine I have mixed"* tells us that to take this journey, **we must be prepared to suffer.**

In Mark 10, James and John come before Jesus, and ask if they can sit beside him on his throne once his kingdom is established. Jesus asks them, *"Are you able to drink the cup I drink?"* They glibly said, *"Yes,"* but they had no idea what they're talking about. Jesus is saying, "Are you ready to follow me on the road to suffering?" (James, incidentally, was the first of the original twelve disciples to be martyred. Be careful what you ask for.)

If you want to learn how to conquer sin and become a more loving, Christlike person, then know up front that suffering will be part of the deal.

Proverbs 9 begins with the words, *"Wisdom has built her house...She has hewn her seven pillars."* The writer compares building a life to building a house. When you come to Christ and give him your life, Jesus is not just going to add on a room to the building of your life, or splash on a fresh coat of religious paint, so that you look good. That's not Christianity. When Jesus comes into your life, he wants to tear your house down to the bare studs and rebuild your life from the ground up.

I like that word 'hewn'. Have you ever split wood? When you swing that ax, you're hewing. And what you do after you hew is you say, "Whew! I could spew some pew!" (To which, some of you are saying, "Ew.")

Hewing is hard work. So is building a life. Building a marriage that is strong and life-giving – takes hard work. Overcoming a nasty habit that's been part of you for years – it's hard. Developing spiritual discipline – not easy. Some people say, "Time heals all wounds." Time heals nothing. It just drives the scars and splinters deeper.

Healing will not come until you say, *"You know what! There's a splinter here, and this has got to come out."* And there'll be screaming and there'll be howling, there'll be spewing while you're hewing, and it will hurt, and you'll want to quit. But for those who have the guts to address the splinter and do what it takes to get it out, Jesus will help them to learn to live in a way they never knew how before.

Building a marriage that lasts, walking away from an addiction, learning how to love – there's nothing harder. It takes real suffering. But it's worth every drop of blood, sweat and tears. Jesus shed the blood. You shed the sweat. And that will bring the beast inside you to heel.

1. Too many Christians have a very weak "theology of suffering". They think that following Christ should be easy and pain-free. Then when suffering comes, they cop an attitude with God. Take five minutes right now, and Google "Bible verses about suffering" then skim the results. Write out three verses that jump off the page for you.

2. What are some truths that you learn from these verses?

Prayer

Through suffering, my Lord, I will grow in character. Through suffering I will prove myself to be an heir with Christ. Through suffering I will develop steadfastness. Through suffering you will burn away my sin, and make me pure. If suffering is part of what it means to live under the Cross, then Lord grant me grace to 'drink of the wine' that you mix for my growth and salvation.

Life Change Requires Repentance

"Come, eat of my bread and drink of the wine I have mixed. Leave your simple ways, and live, and walk in the way of insight." ~ Proverbs 9:5-6

Changing your life for good (for the better), and for good (in a way that lasts) requires coming first to Christ. Then you need God's bread, i.e. his *Word*. Then you need to brace yourself for suffering, for this journey will ask difficult things of you.

Here's one reason why it's hard. This journey requires you to stop doing things you were used to doing, then move your life in a new direction. Which is what the next phrase in Proverbs 9 says: *Leave your simple ways and you will live.*

Christians call this repentance. Repenting isn't just saying, "You're sorry". The abuser who apologizes to his wife but keeps on mistreating her hasn't repented at all. Confession is just the front-half of repenting. The back-half is resolving to live differently.

One author that imprinted on me in seminary was a 16th-century Puritan preacher and writer named Richard Sibbes. Sometimes I find great encouragement pulling up Mr. Sibbes on my Kindle and letting him speak into my life. Recently I was perusing through a sermon he wrote on Hosea 14:1, *"Return, O Israel, to the Lord your God."*

How do we return to God? Sibbes outlined three stages a wandering soul must go through when he or she repents:

"There must be examination and consideration whither our ways tend. There must be stopping considerations."

There must be *stopping considerations.* The language is dated but we get it. (I have a coffee mug with Shakespearean insults on it. I love the phrase: *"You're a bolting hatch of beastliness"*. It's dated, but I get it.)

A "stopping consideration" is when I say to myself, *"I must stop this or this isn't going to turn out well."* The road back to God begins with stopping considerations. Business consultants call it a "bias for action". Until I feel the need to change, I won't.

"There must be humiliation, with displeasure against ourselves...taking shame to ourselves for our ways and courses; and withal, there must concur some hope of mercy."

The *thought* of changing is just the first step. Unless there is some sort of emotional buy-in, we'll not go through with it. *"Blessed are those who mourn,"* Jesus said. Shame is not a bad thing if it sounds off an alarm inside of us that exposes our need for God.

Thirdly, Sibbes writes, *"There must be a resolution to overcome impediments. For when a man thinks or resolves to turn to God, Satan will stir up all his instruments, and labor to kill Christ in his infancy, and to quench good while it is in the purpose only."*

Reflection that leads to remorse is pointless until it prompts a solid resolution to change. The thought *I should return to God* which deepens into *I must return to God* is completed by saying *I will return to God*. With the resolve comes a plan for action, complete with actual steps you will take.

Some of you reading this right now need to repent and return to God. You've wandered far too long, and you're not better off because of it. Listen to the words of this follower of Christ from five centuries ago. Don't be a bolting hatch of beastliness.

1. Is there anything in your life that you are having *stopping considerations* about?

2. What will you do about it?

Prayer

If you've never accepted Christ, a first prayer of repentance might sound like this. For those who are Christians, subsequent prayers of repentance may sound similar. (Just remember when you sin as a Christian, your *relationship* with God remains intact. But your *fellowship* with God may be damaged. For that reason, it's good to come clean with God daily. *"Life is repentance,"* said Martin Luther.)

"Dear God, I know I have sinned in your sight. I have broken your laws and broken your heart by the way I have lived my life. I repent and turn from my sins. I believe Jesus died for my sins, rose from the grave, and is alive right now. I open the door of my heart and life, receiving Jesus Christ as my Savior. I want to follow him as the Lord and Leader of my life. Fill me Holy Spirit of God. Wash away my sins. Teach me and train me to live a new life. Thank you for saving me. Amen."

Life Change Can Happen For You

"Come, eat of my bread and drink of the wine I have mixed. Leave your simple ways, and live, and walk in the way of insight." – Proverbs 9:5-6

For those who come to Christ, who are willing to be nourished by the bread of his Word, and to drink the wine of suffering that must come in following him, and who have learned the grace of regular repentance, a glorious destiny awaits – that soul will come in time to look more like Christ.

You'll begin to *walk in the way of insight*. To "walk in" something means that you're now comfortably settled in with it. It's become second-nature to you because it's now a part of you. This is the very essence of freedom. And when you boil it all down, Christ's came for just this reason – to liberate us. *"If you hold on to my teaching you will know the truth and the truth will set you free,"* Jesus said (John 8:32).

To have sin, any sin, roaming inside of your heart, uncaged and ravenous, is as far from freedom as you can get. To have your soul ruled by greed, or lust, or fear, or unforgiveness, or jealousy, or any of a thousand sins wraps you in terrible chains. The beauty of knowing Christ is that his intent is to break those chains, one by one.

But to reach this place, there are two things about sin you must understand. Your sins must be **forgiven** through repentance (which we talked about in the last devotional), and they must be **unlearned** through training. *"Train yourself to be godly,"* Paul counseled Timothy (1 Timothy 4:7). If I could boil it down to a few steps it might look like this:

Step One: Develop the discipline of meeting with Jesus every day in prayer and the Word, and weekly through fellowship.

Step Two: Pay close attention to what you are hearing, reading and learning. Verses, ideas, thoughts and images will grow in importance in your heart. They'll start to *weigh* on you. These will likely point to things in your life that the Spirit of God is identifying as needing repentance and training.

Step Three: Begin to push back against the behaviors and attitudes that God is bringing up. *This is the part of your healing that will seem painful.* It's easy to do what you've always done. Doing it God's way will seem strange and unnatural at first. You can't do this part alone! Reach out to mentors and spiritual advisors to whom you can be accountable.

Step Four: Celebrate small wins and bring your failures (and there'll be many at first) to Jesus. Remember: *Life is repentance.* Make sure if you hurt someone else with your behavior that you ask for their forgiveness as well.

Step Five: Press forward. Don't give up. Continue meeting with Christ and his people. In time, the tide will turn, and you'll notice a change happening.

Step Six: Make it your #1 goal in life, alongside the exercise and healthy eating and date nights, to meet with Jesus daily in his Word and prayer, and weekly through fellowship. Because once you're "walking in the way of insight" in one area of life, guess what? It'll be time to move on to your next lesson with Jesus.

Step Seven: Never forget that all of this is possible because of the amazing grace of God. Never get too proud of yourself or too down on yourself. Never get too jealous of others for being "stronger than you", or despise others for not being "as far along as you". There's a Cross between us all. Since all of this is possible because of the grace of God, take joy in the journey and worship all the way home.

1. Make sure you have this truth down. My sins must be _____ through repentance, and _____ through training.

2. Learning how to read or listen to God's Word for yourself is an essential life skill. If you struggle with this or are unsure how to do this, make it a top shelf priority to find someone who can teach you this essential discipline. Hopefully, your pastor or other church leaders will be able to quickly point you in the right direction with helpful encouragement and resources.

Prayer

From Psalm 25: To you, O Lord, I lift up my soul. O my God, in you I trust, let me not be put to shame (or make you ashamed.) Make me to know your ways, O Lord; teach me your paths. Lead me in your truth and teach me, for you are the God of my salvation. For you I wait all the day long. Good and upright is the Lord; therefore he instructs sinners in the way. He leads the humble in what is right, and teaches the humble his way.

"Blessed are the meek, for they shall inherit the earth."

Judge Not Knottiness

"Do not give dogs what is holy…Enter by the narrow gate…Beware of false prophets." – Matthew 7:6, 13, 15

It's quite possible that the one verse in the Bible known by more people – believer and unbeliever alike – is Matthew 7:1 – where Jesus says, "Judge not, that you be not judged."

It's also quite possible that no verse in the Bible is more misunderstood, and more misapplied, than this one. How many times have non-Christians hurled this verse back in the face of Christians who try to speak out in favor of biblical morality? "Who do you think you are?! You shouldn't be talking against X, Y or Z. *Judge not!*"

There is a revulsion felt by modern culture to call any given behavior right or wrong. But then look at what modern culture does. Anyone who tries to throw down a boundary is immediately *judged,* as being intolerant, racist, homophobic, hateful, you name it. The ones who scream out the loudest against judging, are themselves masters of it.

Clearly, Jesus is not teaching his followers to suspend all moral judgment and to go through life with an *anything goes* mentality. The very first public word out of Jesus' mouth was *"Repent".* To repent is to admit that something you are doing is harmful or wrong and needs to be repudiated. To repent is to make a judgment.

Right after telling us not to judge, Jesus immediately proceeds to give example after example where his followers *should* make judgments.

- He tells his listeners not to give dogs what is holy or throw their pearls before swine (vs.6), describing a type of listener who is too stubborn or hard-hearted to receive your attempt

to share the gospel.
- He says we are to enter by the narrow gate, for the wide gate leads to destruction (vs.13).
- He warns us to beware of false prophets who come in sheep's clothing (vs.15).
- And to distinguish between trees with good fruit and bad fruit (vs.18-20).
- And to not be hoodwinked by people's words if their actions do not back up what they say (vs.21).
- He tells us to know the difference between a house built on rock as opposed to sand (vss.24-27).

The question becomes: How do you pick out a dog, or pig, a wide gate, a wolf, a tree with bad fruit, or a house on sand *if you do not exercise judgment?*

Obviously, you can't. It sounds to me like Jesus wants his followers to be doing a whole lot of judging, if we're to navigate safely through life.

1. Have you ever been judged for being *judgey*? Or been labeled as "intolerant" by people who think of themselves as "tolerant"? How did you respond?

2. We'll unpack what Jesus means by not judging in the next few devotions. But as you think about it right now, what are your thoughts?

Prayer

Oh Lord, we humans are swayed by outward appearance, while you look on the heart. This whole business of exercising right judgment is beyond me. I need your help. As Paul prayed in Philippians 1:9, may my love abound more and more, with knowledge and all discernment.

When Judging Is The Right Thing To Do

"If anyone is caught in any transgression, you who are spiritual should restore him in a spirit of gentleness." – Galatians 6:1

"Don't judge," Jesus commands in the Sermon on the Mount (Matt.7:1). But he's not telling us to never exercise moral judgment, for that would be foolish, even dangerous. Consider several examples in Scripture where we are told to "judge" the behavior of others.

When someone sins against us. When someone hurts us, Jesus tells us to go to them and point out what they're doing, but to do so privately (Matthew 18:15). We can't say, "Oh, I shouldn't judge. Live and let live." Of course, there are occasions where we need to let things go. The Bible calls that *forbearance.* There's so much sinning to go around, that if we make it our business to point out every time someone nicks us, life will get ugly in a hurry.

How do we know when we should point it out or not? Jesus tells us to go to them with the goal of "gaining our brother or sister back". It's a reconciliation strategy. So if the behavior is something severe enough to hurt the relationship and drive a wedge between you, then it's time to exercise this sort of judgment.

When we see someone caught in a sin. Paul tells us if we see someone *"caught in any transgression"* we should reach out to gently help them. Again, there's a qualifier here. We go to them not when we see them sinning. We're not the moral police, commissioned to go around issuing sin citations for every infraction. God doesn't even do that! *"If you, Lord, kept a record of sins, who could stand?" (Ps.130:3).*

We go to them when we see them *caught* in a sin. Some sin gets on me like mud, and I'm responsible to go to Jesus and get washed off. But some sin wraps around me like a chain, and then the responsibility extends to those around me to help me break free (even though the foolishness for getting caught is all mine.) Strangely, the deeper into sin a person plunges, the more blind to its reality they often become, making it all the more important for those who love them in Christ to exercise moral judgment and go to them.

We are to judge the teaching and character of our leaders. There are two sides to this coin. On the one hand, the Bible tells us *"Obey your leaders and submit to them, for they are keeping watch over your souls"* (Heb.13:17). But a few verses earlier, the writer says, *"Do not be led away by diverse and strange teachings."*

I once read of a pastor caught in adultery, who then announced to his church a week or two later that God had forgiven him so they should as well (translation: *I shouldn't be disciplined for this or be asked to step down.)*

How many thousands of victims of sexual abuse have come forward in recent years with heart-breaking stories of what pastors and leaders did to them? And all because no one around them was judging.

1. Why do you think our instinct when it comes to calling out sin is to not deal with it directly – or perversely, to gossip about it with others?

2. Can you think of a situation you're in right now where God might be asking you to have a difficult conversation with someone else?

Prayer

Our Father, forgive me for the times when I've swept things under the rug which needed to be called out. Yet then there are other times when I've acted like the sin police, full of rage and self-righteousness. I'm quite a mess. Lead me in these oh so complicated areas of life.

A Case Study In Judgmentalism

"Do not judge by appearances, but judge with right judgment." – John 7:24

When Jesus said, "Do not judge, and you will not be judged" he was not telling his followers to unplug their brains and wink at bad behavior.

What does he mean then? Jesus is cutting at the root of a sinful attitude we all struggle with called *judgmentalism*. It's illustrated in a story we read in Luke 7.

Jesus has been invited to the house of a Pharisee name Simon. Midway through the dinner, an intrusion occurs. A woman, whom Luke describes as having *"lived a sinful life"*, barges into the man's house. Without saying a word, the woman begins to cry at Jesus' feet and begins to use her hair as a towel of sorts to wipe them. She then opens up a jar of perfume, which was as expensive back then as it is today (and has caused men from every age to weep and gnash their teeth), then pours it over Jesus' feet.

What offends Simon the Pharisee is not the fact that someone has fallen at Jesus's feet. It's *who this woman is* that disturbs him. And so Simon mutters under his breath, "If this man were a prophet, he would know who is touching him and what kind of woman she is – that she is a sinner."

This is when Jesus turns the table on Simon and exposes his judgmentalism (which now has two layers to it, for Simon is now not only judging the woman, but Jesus as well. Brave man!)

"Simon, I have something to tell you," Jesus says. He proceeds to share with him a story about two men who owe money to a lender. One owes a couple *year's* worth of wages. The other a couple *months*. The lender forgives both debts.

"Which loves the lender more?" Jesus asks Simon. Naturally it was the one forgiven the greater debt. Like this woman here. Jesus could see inside her heart and saw someone who was weary with her life, who wanted desperately to start over, and found in Jesus everything her heart longed for.

"Your sins are forgiven," Jesus says to her.

But Simon saw none of this. He couldn't – because he was filled with ugly judgmentalism. One sign of judgmentalism is this: ***Judgmentalism looks only on the outside, and fails to consider what is in the heart.***

My novel *A Sparrow Could Fall* tells the story of Emma, a woman who is sexually molested by an uncle in her teens. When she inevitably acted out because of the pain and shame she was experiencing, the adults in the church she attended kicked her out, sending her into a decades-long spiral of despair – until she finds healing through the events described in the story.

This is what judgmentalists do. And this is the damage that judgmentalists cause. No one bothered to look inside Emma's heart. All they could see was her outward rebellion. No one bothered to look deeper at the inward pain churning in her heart.

1. Unlike Jesus, we can't see directly into a person's motives. So what might we do to find out what's inside another person's heart? What should the adults around Emma have done?

2. Have you ever been guilty of judging a person solely on the basis of what you saw on the outside?

Prayer

Search me, O God, and know my heart! Try me and know my thoughts! See if there be any grievous way in me, and lead me in the way everlasting! (Psalm 139:23-24)

Two Ways To Know If You're Judgmental

"The Lord is on my side; I will not fear...The Lord is on my side as my helper." – Psalm 118:6-7

In a story from Luke 7, a sinful woman barges in on Jesus while he has dinner in the home of a Pharisee named Simon. Simon's attitude toward the woman reveals a number of traits exhibited by a heart filled with *judgmentalism* – the sin which Jesus condemns when he commands us not to judge. In addition to failing to look inside a person's heart, judgmentalists do this:

Judgmentalists looks at what a person has been, and fail to see what a person can be. Once a sinner, always a sinner. That's a judgmental person's attitude. A judgmental person throws a label on a person. Puts them in a box. To Javert in *Les Miserables*, Valjean will forever be 2-4-6-0-1 (his prisoner number).

Jesus though saw that God's grace could work miracles in a person's life. He could look at a rough and tumble fisherman named Peter and see a man who with some spit and polish could become one of history's most powerful preachers. Jesus could look at a thief dying on the cross and see a man ready for paradise.

What does Jesus see when he looks at you? What can you be, if only grace might be unleashed inside you?

Judgmentalists prefer law over grace. They're always ready to throw the book at people, like Jack Lord from the original *Hawaii 5-0* saying, "Book 'em, Danno!"

"Crucify him! Stone him! Burn him! Kick him out!" has been the cry of judgmentalists throughout the ages. Not that sin doesn't deserve

justice. It does. The wages of sin is death, the Bible says. The problem with judgmentalists is that they are so swift to bring down the hammer, as though they can't wait.

But if there's one thing we learn about God in the Bible, it's that he's not that way at all. God *can* wait, and *does* wait to bring judgment. Psalm 103:8 says, *"The Lord is compassionate and gracious, slow to anger."*

When you see judgment enforced in the Bible, be at the flood of Noah, or the annihilation of the Canaanites, or the exile of Judah, or the fall of Nineveh, or the last days judgment that is yet to fall on the earth, it's understood that God gets no pleasure out of this, and he'd love nothing more than to call off the dogs, if we'd only repent.

And Jesus wants his followers to have this very same spirit. James 2:13 says, *"Judgment without mercy will be shown to anyone who has not been merciful. Mercy triumphs over judgment!"*

Is your heart trending in any of these directions? If so, call to mind all the mercy that God has poured on you in your own life. Let the anti-venom of God's grace work through your own veins. Let it break down the poison of judgmentalism in you.

1. How would you treat a person differently if you looked at them through eyes of faith, and saw what they could be – with Jesus – instead of what they are now?

2. Perhaps your problem is more self-directed. Perhaps you're judgmental against yourself. You don't believe you'll ever change. You see no potential within you. "Once this, always this," you say. "If Jesus looks at me at all, I can only imagine his disappointment." Re-read this devotion and underline or highlight sentences that prove you wrong.

50

Prayer

My Father in heaven, your Word says that you are on my side. In that case, if God is for us then who can be against us? Help me to accept your grace, to believe in your grace, to live in your grace, and then – may I not forget this – to give that grace away to others, and see them through your eyes.

Two More Traits Of Judgmentalism

"Why do you see the speck that is in your brother's eye, but do not notice the log that is in your own eye?" – Matthew 7:3

Two other traits always seem to bubble up in those who have judgmental hearts.

Judgmentalism uses arbitrary standards to judge by. In John 8:1-11 is the story of a woman caught in adultery, then dragged before Jesus by the Pharisees (playing the role of the legalists.) Now what's wrong with this picture?

Where was the man?

But this is what judgmentalists do. They see only the part of the law that they want to see. And remain blind to all the rest. Their standards are arbitrary.

The Pharisees were notorious for this. They got angry at Jesus because he didn't wash his hands the right way, and he healed people on the Sabbath – *the nerve!* – and his disciples didn't fast, and *Who does he think he is calling God his 'Father'?!*

Legalists are still like this today. They judge people by the clothes they wear, or the version of the Bible they read. They pound away on righteousness-sins (like immorality) but ignore justice-sins (like racism). They rail against outward sins, but are oblivious to inward sins such as materialism or pride.

Judgmentalism blinds us to our own sin. I don't think that Jesus was saying to Simon the Pharisee (from the story we considered earlier in Luke 7) that he needed forgiveness any less than the sinful woman. I think in a very subtle, but powerful way, Jesus was suggesting to Simon that he needed to be at Jesus' feet just like she was. But Simon was blind to his own need for God's forgiveness.

On another occasion, Jesus said to a different group of Pharisees, *"It is not the healthy who need a doctor, but the sick. I have not come to call the righteous but sinners to repentance."* (Luke 5:31-32). He wasn't saying that they were healthy. They just thought they were. He wasn't saying that they were righteous. They just thought they were.

Judgmentalism can fool us that way. It's easy to sit in church on Sundays and start to think that we're so much better than everyone out there. It's easy to read the Sunday paper and shake our heads at all the terrible things that people are doing to each other. It's easy to stay in our social media bubble, and start to pat ourselves on the back and think, "Boy, isn't God lucky to have people like me on his side."

Once thoughts like this take root in you, your spiritual eyes become blinded and you become useless to God.

1. Do you have "pet sins" that you see in others which really bring out the thunder from you? Why do these particular sins matter so much to you? Why are you so upset by these, and not others?

2. What point was Jesus making when he compared the sin we see in others to a "speck", but our own sin to a "log"? And why don't we notice this log?

Prayer

Lord God, if I could see the full depth of my sin, all layers of selfishness, hurt and pride which coil around my heart, I think it would cause me to tremble and fall to my knees in horror. Yet how swift I am to figure other people out, or label them, or lash out at them. David was spot-on when he wrote, "Who can discern his errors?" (Psalm 19:12). Forgive me for my foolishness, Lord.

"Blessed are those who hunger and thirst for righteousness, for they shall be satisfied."

Friendship With God Means Seeking Him

"O God, you are my God; earnestly I seek you; my soul thirsts for you; my flesh faints for you, as in a dry and weary land where there is no water." – Psalm 63:1

To live under the Cross will often be a lonely and difficult path to walk. But one comfort along the way is you will have the friendship of God.

The Bible tells us *"The Lord would speak to Moses face to face, as a man speaks with his friend."* (Exodus 33:11). Don't say to yourself, "Well that was Moses! I'm not in his league." Psalm 25:14 tells us, *"The friendship of the Lord is for those who fear him."* So how do you grow in this friendship? Reading further in the story about Moses provides some insight.

The first lesson we learn from Moses about becoming a friend of God is very simple and straightforward. **You have to set your heart to seek God.**

"Now Moses used to take a tent and pitch it outside the camp, far from the camp, and call it the 'tent of meeting'...Whenever Moses went out to the tent, all the people would rise up, and each would stand at his tent door, and watch Moses until he had gone into the tent." (vss.7-8)

The necessity of seeking God is a foundation spiritual truth. *"You will seek me and find me when you seek me with all your heart."* (Jeremiah 29:13). Is God playing some kind of hide and seek game with us? Why do we have to do this?

Because this is how we show God the seriousness of our hearts. Thousands of people followed Jesus at first, riding the wave of his popularity. Jesus would withdraw – a few would stop following, but the others would come and find him. He'd walk across (not around) a lake; a smaller group would jump in their boats and follow.

He'd say things to put them off his scent. A Canaanite woman sought him once, seeking healing for her sick daughter. Jesus said to her, *"Woman, I was sent only to the lost sheep of Israel. It's not right to take the children's bread and toss it to the dogs."* Why'd he do this? It sounds cruel. But he was probing her heart, trying to draw out her faith.

So when the Canaanite woman cried out to him, *"Yes Lord, but even the dogs eat the crumbs that fall from their master's table"*, he knew that here was a woman that would not let go of God, no matter what (Matthew 15:22-28). And Jesus rewarded her seeking.

Will you take hold of God with that kind of intensity and passion? Moses set the tent of meeting *"some distance away"* from the camp. When Jesus would go to pray, Scripture tells us he would often withdraw to desolate, lonely places (Luke 5:16). Why? Seeking God is serious business. Though it is birthed in grace, real effort in required on our parts.

You can't just stay inside the doorway of your tent and expect to have a deeper experience of God.

1. Think of three things you can do in the next month to seek God with greater focus.

2. Conduct a prayer experiment today. Pray aloud Psalm 63:1 now, then several times through. Then try to call it to mind and say it at least once *each waking hour* throughout the day. Then write down some observations you make about this prayer experiment.

57

Prayer

O God, you are my God. Be present in my thoughts all day long. Give me spiritual tenacity like that Canaanite woman to pursue you and not let go. Can I honestly say like David that I thirst for you? And faint for you? Help the fire of my faith in Christ grow brighter and stronger.

Friendship With God Means Listening

"The heavens declare the glory of God, and the sky above proclaims his handiwork. Day to day pours out speech." – Psalm 19:1-2

What a friend we have in Jesus, that great old hymn declares. So how do we nurture this friendship? A second lesson we learn from Moses' friendship with God is **Moses allowed God speak into his life.**

Exodus 33:9 says, *"When Moses entered the tent, the pillar of cloud would descend and stand at the entrance of the tent, and the Lord would speak with Moses."*

Most people think of prayer as you speaking with God, but we mustn't forget that prayer is also God speaking with you. There is a listening component to prayer which cannot be overlooked. If in prayer we do all the talking, then we have not prayed.

God says to us in Psalm 46:10, *"Be still and know that I am God."* The prophet Isaiah told us where we'd find our strength. *"In quietness and trust shall be your strength."* (Isaiah 30:15). Jesus told us in John 10:27, *"My sheep hear my voice, and I know them, and they follow me."*

Most people who treat Christianity as more a religion than a relationship never allow God to get a word in edgewise. Much of this is intentional. Because once you start letting God speak to you about your life, he's going to start meddling. And tinkering. And pointing out things you'd rather not deal with. So you put a muzzle on God, or you stop up your ears. Religion is so much more comfortable. And safer too.

But for those who want to be friends with God, they will leave margins of quietness in which God might speak. They will say, like Samuel, *"Speak Lord, your servant is listening."* And often God will do just that.

How can I learn to hear God's voice?

It begins by letting God speak to you through His Word. He will speak to you in the act of having your quiet time (which is why it's a life-giving goal to develop the habit of a *daily* devotion).

When your ears and heart are open to God, and you learn to study Scripture properly, words will start to leap off the page for you. Images of things, and quiet whispers too, will enter your mind. They'll be things that you probably wouldn't have imagined all on your own – that will have the aroma of Jesus about them.

Another important way God speaks into our lives is through other people, particularly our Christian brothers and sisters. Through something as sublime as a sermon, or as simple as a cup of coffee or tea with a friend, God can speak to you concerning things that occupy your 'blind spot' – things you wouldn't see or think about unless someone else called attention to them.

1. Has God ever spoken to you through a Bible verse, a sermon, a friend, or a thought? Describe it.

2. How much quietness do you leave in your day-to-day life? Is there anything you can tweak to make room for more stillness?

Prayer

My Jesus, I love Thee; I know Thou art mine. Such intimacy is heard in the words of this hymn, my Lord. Would you grant me the grace of hearing your voice? Help me to tune down the noise in my life, and to stop treating my faith as mere religion, when you are offering a relationship.

Friendship With God Means Knowing Him

"And this is eternal life; that they know you the only true God, and Jesus Christ whom you have sent." – John 17:3

Another thing that stands out about Moses and the friendship he enjoyed with God in Exodus 33 is that he wasn't content to remain where he was at. He wanted to grow. Which is a lesson for those who become God's friends. **They long to know God more.**

Two verses after telling us the Lord spoke to Moses as a man to his friend, Moses says to God, *"If you are pleased with me, teach me your ways so I may know you and continue to find favor with you."* (Exodus 33:13).

Moses is hungry like a desperate beggar for more of God. Jesus made a beautiful promise concerning those who seek God with this sort of holy desperation. *"Blessed are those who hunger and thirst for righteousness, for they shall be satisfied."* (Matt.5:6).

As we look through Scripture, it appears at first glance that God is closer to some than others. Among Jesus' twelve disciples, there was the inner circle of Peter, James, and John, and among the Three, John was known as *the disciple Jesus loved.*

You may say, *It's not fair. God's playing favorites.* But it has nothing at all to do with God playing favorites. *"God shows no partiality,"* Paul says (Galatians 2:6). It's simply God's response to hearts that hunger for more of him. We find John sitting right next to Jesus at the Last Supper. And when the others denied, betrayed and fled Jesus in his sufferings, it was John who stood right there under the Cross.

Some people think pastors are closer to God than others. Not true.

Some people think those who have been Christians for a long time are closer to God than others. Wrong again. Age does not guarantee maturity. Psalm 119:100 says, *"I understand more than the aged, for I keep your precepts."*

This has nothing to do with your age, or your intellect. It has all to do with your heart.

So how do you grow in knowing God? I read recently that an 18th-century Spanish galleon with as much as $17 billion in gold was discovered off the coast of Columbia. This wasn't just lucky. It was the result of an all-out search. Guess what? The Bible says that growing in the knowledge of God is just like that.

Proverbs 2:3-5 says, *"If you call out for insight...if you look for it as for silver and search for I as for hidden treasure, then you will understand the fear of the Lord and find the knowledge of God."*

Do you have the deep desire to know God more and more? This is the born-again birthright for any child of God. Paul writes in Ephesians 1:17, *"I keep asking God...that you may know him better."*

Those whom God brings into his inner circle of friendship have this hunger. Do you?

1. Take a moment to think about where you would like to be as a follower of Christ five years from now. If you could sit down and have coffee with yourself, describe the Future You.

2. What are some things the Future You probably did in those preceding five years to get to that place?

Prayer

Dear Savior, you compared yourself in John 15 to a vine, and described me as a branch. Then you promised if I would remain attached to you, that you would make me increasingly fruitful. I desire this, my Lord. I want to know you more. I want my life to reflect more of your love and goodness. Give me grace to grab hold of you, hang on tight, and go where you would lead me.

Friendship With God Means Pleasing Him

"So whether we are at home or away, we make it our aim to please him." – 2 Corinthians 5:9

Because he was God's friend, Moses' instinct was to **please God.**

In Exodus 33:14-17, Moses prays for God to go with Israel as she enters into the Promised Land. *"Then Moses said to him, 'If your Presence does not go with us, do not send us up from here. How will anyone know that you are pleased with me and with your people unless you go with us...And the Lord said to Moses, 'I will do the very thing you have asked, because I am pleased with you and I know you by name.'"*

You cannot claim to be God's friend if you have no concern for pleasing God with your life. Ephesians 5:10 tells us *"Find out what pleases the Lord."* Sounds simple enough, but not every Christian has this mindset.

I was talking to someone once who was struggling with a moral dilemma. They more or less came to me looking for a pastoral blessing on a bad choice they were about to make. And the thing was, they knew what was right and wrong in this situation! In fact, this person said at very beginning of the conversation, "Look, I know as a Christian that the hard way is usually the God way."

Then they proceeded to beg me to help them take the easy way out. Well, physician, heal thyself! Clearly, this person's instinct was not to please the Lord, but to satisfy their own self-centered desires.

I thought what this person said was fascinating. *"The hard way is usually the God way."* Jesus said as much. *"Wide is the gate and broad is the road that leads to destruction, and many enter through it. But small is the gate and narrow the road that leads to life, and only a few find it."* (Matt.7:13-14).

It's easier to want the divorce than work on the marriage. It's easier to cave in to the temptation than to fight it. It's easier to go along with the crowd than to be the one who stands out by making the right choice. It's easier to point fingers and blame the other person for your relationship struggles than try to listen, forgive, and do the hard work of reconciliation.

The hard way is usually the God way, and also – don't forget this – *it's the best way.*

But here's the good news. Though it's the hard way, we *don't have to do it on our own.* To live under the Cross is to agree with God that we're powerless to live a life that pleases him on our own. For those who own up to their weakness and sin, Jesus himself will come alongside us to walk the journey of life.

Cry out to him today. Seek him. Listen to him. Yield to him. His arms are open wide. And his friendship is for you.

1. *Find out what pleases the Lord.* List 2 or 3 specific ways to do this.

2. *The hard way is usually the God way.* If I discover that I'm doing something that pleases me but doesn't please God, what will happen next? Who will win the tug of war?

66

Prayer

Holy Spirit, your intent is to make me holy. You're not the Happiness Spirit. Or the Success Spirit. This means that there will likely be times when my sinful self will want to buck, and pull back on the reins. I invite you to break me, and train me, and give me a heart for pleasing my Master.

Friendship With God: It Takes Time To Grow

"Like newborn infants, long for the pure spiritual milk, that by it you may grow up into salvation." – 1 Peter 2:2

Leonard Ravenhill told the story of a group of tourists vacationing in England, who were walking through a little village one day. They passed an old man sitting in a park, and one of the tourists, being a wise guy, called out, "Old chap, were any great men born in this village?" The old man replied, "Nope, only babies."

It's true for all of us. Sometimes we look at the Bible and we see Moses' friendship with God, David's love of God, Esther's courage for God, Paul's trust in God, and rather than be inspired by them, we're intimidated. They're so far above us, we think. But that's not true.

Each one of them started off as spiritual babies. Each one of them began with the seed of faith being planted in his or her heart, and that seed had to watered, weeded and cared for. Just like with the seed that's in you. Living under the Cross places before us the opportunity to grow.

I remember in college talking to a pastor I knew, and someone walked up and said, "Oh Pastor, I'm blown away by how well you know Scripture." And it was true - you could say two words of a verse to him, and he'd tell you where it was found without hesitation. It awed me, but also inspired me to keep up my own Bible reading. Years later, I was shaking hands with folks in my church after preaching, and someone came up and said, "Oh Pastor, I'm blown away by how well you know Scripture."

Suddenly I remembered that little moment from so long before. And smiled a prayer of thanks to God that he had given me the grace to keep my nose in the book, day after day, and year after year. Without hardly even noticing it, the seed in me had grown.

One of the things that encourages me when I read the Bible is to realize how many of the great heroes of faith arose out of obscurity, after spending years hidden away.

Before Moses marched into the royal hall in Egypt to face down Pharaoh, he spent forty years herding sheep. Before David conquered Goliath, he was the runt of the litter, writing songs that he was sure no one would hear. Esther was a nobody who won a beauty contest. Before Paul began his prolific missionary career, he spent more than fifteen years out of the limelight in his hometown of Tarsus.

What were they doing during these years? Just faithfully serving and seeking the Lord. Worshipping. Staying in fellowship. Studying God's Word. Doing ministry. Fighting off sin. Telling others about the God they loved. And with them scarcely noticing, the seed of faith in them was *growing.*

Were any great men and women born in your church? Nope. Only babies. Babies in whom a wonderful seed gets planted. The greatness comes by nurturing that seed.

1. Write down 3-5 things that must be true if a person enters God's kingdom as a spiritual baby.

2. Why do you think some people stay stuck in place after their conversion? What hinders them from growing?

Prayer

My Father, by grace you have made me your child. But it is your desire that I grow up into salvation. Give me holy tenacity to grow in the grace and knowledge of my Lord and Savior (2 Peter 3:18). May I be rooted and built up in Christ, and established in the faith (Col.2:7).

"Blessed are the merciful, for they shall receive mercy."

Love Your Enemies? Some Objections

"Love your enemies and pray for those who persecute you, so that you may be sons of your Father who is in heaven." – Matthew 5:44-45

If you thought the Lord's words about judging were difficult to hear, now we come to perhaps the his most absurd, insane admonition – to love our enemies.

What's your first reaction to these words? Isn't there part of you that wants to say, *"But Lord if we do that, they'll get away with it." "But Lord, if we do that, they'll walk all over us."*

It flies in the face of reason. Our world tells us that when someone hits us, we've got to hit back and hit back harder, or the bully won't stop. It defies human nature. We love it when Harrison Ford snarls, "Get off my plane!" then sends the bad guy hurling 30,000 feet to meet his Maker.

Before we talk about how this teaching might be lived out, let's first address some objections. One objection is, **It's impossible to love my enemies.** If ever we needed proof that to live under the Cross is a hopeless ideal unless the Lord gives us grace, it is here.

But the simple fact of the matter is for the first three centuries of the church's history, the early Christians *did* live this way. Islam was spread in the sixth century by Mohammed's armies. Conversions were made at swordpoint. It continues to this day. But with Christianity, it was different. The followers of Jesus carried no swords. They formed no terrorist networks. The pagan philosopher Celsus complained that if everyone became a Christian there would be no army. Yet Christianity grew exponentially.

A second objection is that **loving your enemies doesn't work**. If we act this way, it won't solve the problem of evil.

Prime Minister Chamberlain of England and the other European powers capitulated to Hitler time and time again, allowing him to only grow more ruthless. Look at the locusts in *"A Bug's Life"*. Until the ants put their feet down – all six of them – the locusts pushed them around like...well, bugs. What do the righteous have to do to allow evil to spread? All together now: *Nothing!*

However, let's not put words in Jesus' mouth. He's not telling us to let people get away with evil. Or do nothing. Or say nothing. We *are* to respond to evil. But what Jesus is teaching us is to respond to it in a different way than our feelings and out culture is telling us to. And Jesus' way, while not easy, does work.

The early Christians' example of loving their enemies caused the hope and freedom of the gospel to spread like wildfire throughout the Roman empire. *"We're everywhere!"* the third century writer Tertullian boasted to the pagan Romans. *"We're in your shops, we're in your marketplaces, we fill your cities, and towns and countryside, the only thing we've left you is your temples, and you can have them. The more you mow us down, the more we grow, for the blood of martyrs is seed."*

Two millennia later, men like Gandhi and Martin Luther King, Jr., changed their respective worlds by adopting Christ's impossible, unworkable teaching. And so can you.

1. Why is the remarkable growth of Christianity in its first three centuries proof of the truthfulness of our faith?

2. Be honest. When you hear the Lord say, "Love your enemies", how do you respond?

Prayer

My loving God, I'm going out into a world today that is filled with an overwhelming amount of hatred and fear. I'll see it on the roads. I'll see it at work or at school. I'll see it in social media and on the news. Though I don't know how, use me this day to spread your love in some way. Some how, some way, help me to tamp down the hatred that lurks in my part of the world.

Love Your Enemies? Some Conditions

"Rescue those being taken away to death; hold back those who are stumbling to the slaughter." – Proverbs 24:11

Christ's teaching that his followers love their enemies is arguably one of the most difficult of his commands to process, let alone obey. An enemy means a bully, an abuser, a swindler, a terrorist, the spouse who abandoned us (and these days a member of the other political party.)

Looking at the example of the early church however, we observe some qualifications of what it means to love one's enemy. And when we see it play out in real-time, what we notice is it's as far from weakness as can be. It is in fact the height of moral strength.

It doesn't mean we don't speak out against evil.
The Bible tells us to speak the truth in love. We see the early Christians confronting the evil they faced time and time again. Evil needs to be exposed as evil with all the conviction and passion we can muster. Jesus spoke truth to power at his own trial. Only at the end did he button up and refuse to play the game anymore with his accusers.

The apostle Paul spoke loudly and clearly in his own defense at his many interrogations and trials. The early church fathers wrote blistering articles and books addressed to the Roman authorities, protesting the way Christians were being treated.

Gandhi, a practitioner of nonviolence, wrote: *"Nonviolence does not mean meek submission to the will of the evildoer, but it means putting one's whole soul against the will of the tyrant."*

It doesn't mean we don't take full advantage of every legal recourse at our disposal in fighting evil.

Paul was falsely accused and arrested by his Jewish opponents. Did he just turn the other cheek and accept their punishment? No – he appealed to the Roman authorities, and eventually Caesar himself. As a Roman citizen, Paul had certain rights which the law gave him, and more than once, Paul played this card to his advantage.

As we struggle against evil in our society, we are privileged with tremendous resources of freedom and legal recourse in America. Particularly as religious liberty comes under siege in our culture today, we need to make full use of the power at our disposal. We must also use that power to come to the defense of our suffering brothers and sisters around the world.

It doesn't mean we hang onto violence as a last resort if everything else fails.
We find in the example of the early church that when their speaking failed, and when every legal recourse dried up, even when the law turned against them, Christian refused to do two things*: 1) They refused to compromise their faith, and 2) they refused to resort to violence to find vindication, but accepted whatever mistreatment was given them.*

The Jewish leaders told Peter and John, "We order you to stop preaching in Jesus' name." Peter and John shrugged their shoulders and said, "We must obey God rather than men." Yet when they were beaten and imprisoned for breaking the law, they accepted the mistreatment. In fact, the Bible says they rejoiced that they were counted worthy to suffer for Jesus (Acts 5:41).

Have no doubt about it. Every suicide bomber, every person who has ever bombed an abortion clinic, or planted a burning cross in someone's lawn, or looted a neighborhood in "protest" at police brutality, or threatened college students for inviting a speaker they might disagree with – these are nothing but moral cowards, a million miles away from the heart of our Savior.

1. How can you "put one's whole soul against the will of the tyrant" without resorting to violence? What did Gandhi mean?

2. What would you say to a wife being abused by a husband, who tells you, "But I must submit to him, you know. Christ calls me to love him."

Prayer

Spirit of God, I ask you for wisdom in how to follow my Lord's example in loving my enemies. Even if right now, I don't experience hatred in my own personal life, your people are facing it all around me in the wider world. And maybe I need to use my position of freedom and strength to help them. To those who are given much, much is expected. Show me how.

Love Your Enemies: Bless Them, Don't Curse

"A soft answer turns away wrath, but a harsh word stirs up anger. The tongue of the wise commends knowledge, but the mouths of fools pours out folly." – Proverbs 15:1

There's a lot of hatred spewing out in our world these days. It's like a soda can that's been shaken up, and then the top gets ripped off. Jesus said in the last days of earth, *"because lawlessness will be increased, the love of many will grow cold"* (Matthew 24:12). Could this be us? Is there any way to get this genie of hatred back into the bottle?

As a matter of fact, there is a group of people walking the earth today who have been given a command from their leader to show the world that another way is possible. We call them Christians; they follow the one called Jesus Christ; and Jesus gave his followers this command: *"Love your enemies."*

So what is Jesus telling us specifically to do here? Here's one idea. Loving my enemy means: **I will watch the way I speak of my enemy. My enemy is someone worth understanding.**

Jesus tells us, *"Bless those who persecute you; bless and do not curse."* The first step of hatred is to dehumanize my enemy, and we typically do this with words. We do it when we're gossiping at the coffee pot. *"Did you hear what that moron boss of ours did the other day?"* We do it when we rage at others when engaged in bumper to bumper combat on the road. *"Use your signal you idiot!"* Parents do it when they yell at their kids at a vein-popping volume. Name-calling has become a populist art form today in our politics.

But Jesus says to us in so many words, *Don't lose sight of the humanity of your enemy.* So tone down the venom. Try blessing them instead. I mean, honestly, do we really think our fuming and fist-shaking will cause the other person to say, "Oh my. I didn't realize how my behavior was so hurtful. I'd best change. Thank you for yelling at me!"

Back in the late 80s, my wife and I spent a year in inner city London serving a church there with a couple of remarkable Christians. Paul and his wife Helen had the most contagious love for the people living in the church's neighborhood.

One day, Paul and I were walking across a playground, standing in the shadows of the oppressive, prison-like government housing projects that surrounded us. We came across a group of kids who were breaking empty beer bottles against a wall. Anger welled up within me. Obviously, they needed discipline and I would be the Lord's messenger to provide it.

But before I could scold them, Paul stopped, and with a sympathetic smile, said, "You boys are kind of bored today, aren't you?" He saw past the behavior, and saw their humanity. It jumpstarted a short conversation with them, in which Paul was able to plant a few Jesus-seeds into their hearts.

Paul taught me how to insert a prayerful pause into my interactions with the sin-sick souls I meet. People who live under the Cross will do this.

The high school punk walks past, with orange and blue hair, a cigarette dangling from his lips, with a cocky grin I want to punch from his face. Here I insert the prayerful pause. Suddenly I see something else. I see the little boy whose father abandoned him, and whose mother taught him nothing but profanity, and a bleeding, wounded spirit that's never been loved, and needs Jesus desperately.

Now God has something to work with.

1. What might be the story behind the: drug addict? thief? terrorist? homeless man? transgender person? Republican/Democrat?

2. What would it take for you when you cross paths with someone to whom you want to read the riot-act, to instead say to them in words of your choosing, "Bless you"?

Prayer

God, you showed your boundless love for me in that, while I was still a sinner, Christ died for me. And while I was still lost, saying and thinking terrible things about you, still you pursued me and called out to me. Help me to love the sin-stuck around me with that same radical, reckless love.

Love Your Enemies: Forgiveness (What It's Not)

"And Jesus said, 'Father, forgive them, for they know not what they do.'" – Luke 23:34

In 2018, the US federal government reopened its investigation into the grisly 1955 murder of 14-year-old Emmett Till. Emmett, a playful African-American teen from Chicago, was visiting relatives in Mississippi. He and some friends had just walked out of a store, when one of his buddies asked if he liked the white lady at the cash register.

Accounts vary on what happened, but it's believed that Emmett whistled boisterously, which was overheard by a white customer. A few days later, Emmett was kidnapped, and his disfigured, tortured body was found in a river shortly afterwards. His death became a flashpoint across the nation for advancing the Civil Rights movement.

Years later, Emmett's mother Mamie was asked if she harbored any bitterness toward her son's killers. She said, *"What they had done was not for me to punish and it was not for me to go around hugging hatred to myself, for hate would destroy me. And it wouldn't hurt them."*

I have a hard time imagining myself saying similar words if I were in her situation. But Mamie's response illuminates the power of forgiveness, which is another aspect of what Jesus meant when he told his followers to love their enemies.

And if Mamie's words are jarring, Jesus' words spoken *from the cross,* to the ones who crucified him, and were mocking him, and were gambling for his clothes, *as he spoke the words,* are even more incomprehensible.

C.S. Lewis wrote, *"Everyone thinks forgiveness is a lovely idea, until they have something to forgive."*

One necessary starting place when talking about forgiveness is to understand *what it is not.* These are just bullet-points of massive ideas which have taken others volumes to unpack. *Forgiveness is not:*

Forgetting. There is no lobotomy of the mind that can excise the memories of the Holocaust. Or the horrors of sexual abuse. Or the atrocities of war.

Excusing. We're afraid that if we forgive someone, then their sin against us will be seen as *not that bad.* But what they did is just as wrong the moment before I forgive as the moment after.

Trusting. If you're abusive or an addict, I can forgive you, but I would be a fool to return to square one with you. Forgiveness doesn't ask that we trust the untrustworthy. Behavior has consequences which need to be worked through.

Letting yourself be trampled on. A few years ago, a pastor in the town where I lived was killed when a mentally ill man assaulted him. Put in a similar situation, I would not turn the other cheek, I assure you. Or if I came across someone assaulting another person, I would not walk away. If a wild animal breaks into my house, I'll do everything and anything to protect my family from that animal. A lawless home-invader or assailant is no different than a wild animal in this respect.

1. Can you think of a time when you found it difficult to forgive someone? Describe it.

2. What is it that makes forgiveness so difficult?

82

Prayer

"Forgive us our trespasses as we forgive those who trespass against us." I let these words flow so effortlessly from my tongue, Lord, but I'm not so sure if I've ever fully grasped what it is I'm saying. Give me grace not to hug hatred to myself.

Love Your Enemies: Forgiveness (What It Is)

"Be kind to one another, tenderhearted, forgiving one another, as God in Christ forgave you." – Ephesians 4:32

In the timeless story *Les Miserables,* Jean Valjean has just been released from prison, where he has served time for stealing bread. He has no money, and he spends his first night out of prison in the home of a village priest who takes him in. In the night, Jean Valjean flees the priest's home after assaulting him and stealing most of his valuable silverware. But he is captured and the police bring him back to the priest so that he can be formally accused.

For Jean Valjean, this means his last hope is gone. He will now be imprisoned for the rest of his miserable life. The priest comes to him and looks him in the eyes, and says, "My brother, why did you leave so quickly last night? You took only the silver. But I gave you these as well." And he places in his hands several more golden candlesticks.

The priest had the right to ask for justice. But he saw something worth saving in this thief, and gave forgiveness instead. That moment changed Jean Valjean's life.

Forgiveness has that kind of power. Having shared some thoughts about what forgiveness is not, it's important to attempt a description of what it is. *Forgiveness is:*

Letting go of the desire to pay back or get even. Romans 12:17 says, *"Do not repay anyone evil for evil...Do not take revenge...but leave room for God's wrath."* God sees it all. This one thought can end feuds and shatter generational cycles of violence.

A prominent social scientist once wrote: *"Forgiveness represents the most strategic intervention in reducing violence in our society."* Can you imagine what would happen if this one verse were put into practice in the Middle East, or in the troubled parts of Africa, or in an urban neighborhood, or in your family?

This kind of forgiveness can save society.

Letting go of the anger and bitterness raging inside of us. Holocaust survivor Claude Lanzman wrote, *"If you could lick my heart, it would poison you."* This was what Emmett Till's mother Mamie meant when she said, *"I can't go hugging hatred to myself."*

Clara Barton, the founder of the Red Cross, was once reminded by a friend of a cruel thing that someone had done to her, but she seemed to not remember it. "Oh come on, Clara," said her friend. "You surely can't forget something like that." "On the contrary," Clara replied. "I distinctly remember forgetting it." Forgiveness does not mean forgetting a memory. But forgiveness does mean defanging a memory, before it devours us from the inside out.

This kind of forgiveness can save me.

Seeing something redemptive in the other person and letting them live again. This is what the priest saw in Valjean. And this is what Christ saw in his executioners.

It's mind-blowing when you think about it. In saying from the cross, *"Father, forgive them; they know not what they're doing,"* Jesus was considering in real-time the backstory to each of the soldiers. In a glimpse, he took in their family of origin, their culture, their education, their birth order, their IQ, their EQ, and a thousand other variables that led them to behave as they did in this moment. *All of that* Jesus pardoned before heaven, so that should any of them one day see things differently, or outgrow their ignorance, or discover the truth of who he was, they could have a relationship with him, no questions asked, and live again.

It would be like a person losing a loved one to a terrorist act, then at the trial of the terrorist, looking on him, and not seeing the defiant, vain murderer, but suddenly seeing a little boy growing up in a shanty town in in Pakistan, thrust into a school at the age of three, where hate-mongering clerics forced him to chant verses from the Koran along with anti-Western slogans, then saying at his sentencing, "I forgive you."

This kind of forgiveness can save the sinner.

And dear ones, *this* is the kind of forgiveness that God has given you and me in Christ.

1. Re-read the theme verse for this reading. Write a sentence or two which describes how much sinning you have done in your life. Think in terms of quantity, and weight, and impact.

2. Re-read the theme verse once again. Write a sentence of two which describes why you should practice forgiveness with others.

Prayer

God in heaven, I do not deserve to know you as a Father. I do not deserve admittance into your kingdom. I do not deserve to be called your son or daughter. But all this you have given me freely in Christ, and a thousand blessings more. He who has been forgiven much, loves much. Help me to love you and love others in measure with the forgiveness you have poured out on me.

"Blessed are the pure in heart, for they shall see God."

The Cycle Of Sin: Desire

"The heart is deceitful above all things, and desperately sick. Who can understand it?" – Jeremiah 17:9

That human beings are morally flawed should be one of the more obvious truths about us. The most popular TV shows of the early 21st-century – from *Walking Dead* to *Breaking Bad* to *This Is Us* love to explore the twisted depths of the human heart.

But why are we by nature "bad"? It's important that we answer this correctly, for the right diagnosis leads to the right treatment. A faulty diagnosis leads to mischief, or worse.

James 1:14-15 provides helpful insight. *"Each person is tempted when he is lured and enticed by his own desire. Then desire when it has conceived gives birth to sin, and sin when it is fully grown brings forth death."* This passage describes what we might call the "cycle of sin". Notice where our moral failures begin – with an evil desire that resides inside of us.

It's commonly believed that humans are essentially good, and that the reason we break bad is because of external problems that must be fixed. I'm all for fixing external problems. It's part of the stewardship that God asks humans to exercise over the earth.

Education, yes. A solid economy, bring it. Fight injustice, everywhere you find it. But let's not pretend that this alone is our golden ticket to Valhalla.

After World War II, Great Britain organized a massive rebuilding project that provided affordable government housing to its urban population. While living in London a few years ago, I saw with my own eyes how many of these planned communities had turned into nightmarish concrete jungles of despair and crime in less than a generation.

Remove the heel of the tyrant's oppression from off of the necks of the Iraqi, the Egyptian, the Libyan...and it was believed an "Arab spring" would ensue. Instead, the Middle East has become a quagmire of terrorism and chaos.

Modern day experts point to all sorts of exterior things that need to be fixed, silenced or removed from office if our world is ever to improve. It's Hollywood, it's the liberal press, it's those hateful Christians, it's global warming...

No, Jesus says, *the problem doesn't start out there. The problem begins in our hearts.*

Mark 7:20 – *"For from within, out of men's hearts, come evil thoughts, sexual immorality, theft, murder, adultery, greed, malice, deceit, lewdness, envy, slander, arrogance and folly. All these evils come from inside and make a man unclean."*

When your car misfires, go ahead and wash it and wax it if you want, but until you raise the hood and poke around with what's inside, you won't fix the problem.

If something is misfiring in your life right now, you can blame your spouse, your boss, or a thousand other things if you want. Here's a thought. Find a mirror somewhere close, and take a good, long look at what's staring back.

Let's start by fixing what we see there first.

1. Let's say we acquire the technology to colonize Mars safely. For the first colonists, let's then say we choose a hundred of the most

intelligent, moral, ethical, upstanding humans on the planet. It's a veritable paradise. If Jesus is correct about the human heart, what do you think we'd find on Mars a hundred years after this promising beginning?

2. Do you agree or disagree with the biblical assessment that the heart of the human problem is the problem of the human heart? Explain your answer.

Prayer

O Lord, hide your face from my sins, and blot out all my iniquities. Create in me a clean heart, O God, and renew a right spirit within me. Cast me not away from your presence, and take not your Holy Spirit from me. (from Psalm 51)

The Cycle Of Sin: Deception

"But I am afraid that as the serpent deceived Eve by his cunning, your thoughts will be led astray from a sincere and pure devotion to Christ."
– 2 Corinthians 11:3

King David walked out on his roof one starry night – to pray, to play his lyre, to binge-watch some TV, no one knows. But across the way, he saw a woman bathing. She was beautiful, and at once David felt the machinery of his masculinity swing into motion.

The cycle of sin which James 1:13-15 describes begins with *desire*. *"Each person is tempted when he is lured and enticed by his own desire."* Yet notice – desire is not sin.

David's sexual desire is a God-given and good gift God has given to the human race. What David felt the first instant he looked at Bathsheba was the firing of attraction and longings which were normal parts of his humanity. What makes sin *sin* is fulfilling those good desires in ways which God prohibits.

Because God loves us, he puts boundaries around our desires and behaviors, not to stifle our happiness, but to insure it. Notice then where temptation meets us – at the point where our *desires* meet up with God's *boundaries*. It's at that point of intersection that we feel the sting of temptation.

And if we let temptation linger and gnaw on us rather than chase it away at step one, then we proceed to step two in the cycle of sin – *deception*. The more we loiter at temptation's doorstep, the more our mind begins to question God's boundaries.

Satan comes to Adam and Eve in the Garden and says, *"Did God really say, 'You must not eat from any tree in the garden'?"* Eve starts to talk to him. Big mistake! The devil can out-talk you, out-argue you, out-smart you, out-persuade you every time. He's had a lot more practice than you.

David knew what God's boundaries were when he saw Bathsheba. But the very next verse of the story says, *"David sent someone to find out about her"* (2 Samuel 11:3). This is David telling the devil, "Hey, grab yourself a cup of coffee, pull up a chair, let's talk about this."

What's interesting is David's messenger comes back and says to David, *"This is Bathsheba...the wife of Uriah the Hittite."* David is given one more chance to come to his senses. *She's the wife of another man, David! The boundaries, David! Hello!*

God always comes to us in that moment when the deception occurs. That much he promises us. 1 Corinthians 10:13 says, *"God is faithful; he will not let you be tempted beyond what you can bear. But when you are tempted, he will also provide a way out so that you can stand up under it."* In the darkest moment of temptation when the deception seems greatest, and your doubt is churning, God is there.

The next move is yours.

1. Someone once said that when we *rationalize* our wrong choices, we use *rational lies*. What does this mean?

2. Can you think of a time when in the midst of a temptation, God provided an escape hatch for you? Did you take it?

Prayer

It's interesting Lord Jesus how in the Lord's Prayer you teach us to use the words, 'Lead me not into temptation'. It's as if you already know how weak I am. And better to not even face temptation, because once I get in its crosshairs it's hard to get out. Lord, train me to be godly. I ask you, God of peace, to sanctify me completely. May my whole spirit and soul and body be kept blameless before you. (1 Timothy 4:7; 1 Thess.5:23)

The Cycle Of Sin: Disobedience

"Each person is tempted when he is lured and enticed by his own desire. Then desire when it has conceived gives birth to sin, and sin when it is fully grown brings forth death." – James 1:14-15

King David in his sordid affair with Bathsheba illustrates the cycle of sin. Sin begins with desires that churn inside our heart. The desire itself may be harmless at first. David unexpectedly caught a glimpse of Bathsheba bathing, and it stirred his God-given sexual desires. Living in this sex-saturated world, this happens to us all the time.

Temptation is best managed in the desire stage, because it's still just a bud of a thought, which with a little discipline and self-control, is easy to nip. At least "easy" compared to what comes next.

The second stage of the cycle of sin is "deception", where rather than snuffing that desire out like a bad cigarette, we chum with it. "Let's talk," we say. Which desire loves to do. It will begin to pitch you all the reasons why we should fulfill its wishes. And why the boundaries God has set around it are so over-the-top and unnecessary.

Temptation is harder to fight here because now we must summon reasons in our heart why obedience is best. David asks some of his men who the woman is. One speaks up. *"David, she's the wife of Uriah the Hittite."* That was David's escape hatch. With those words, David should have realized his vulnerability. It would have been a good time to write a psalm. Or put out a 911 to Nathan the prophet.

But the very next words in the story are heart-sickening. *"Then David sent messengers to get her. She came to him, and he slept with her."* (2 Samuel 11:4).

Step three in the cycle of sin is **disobedience.** *"Then, after desire has conceived, it gives birth to sin,"* James says.

What this passage teaches is that our sinning is not a spontaneous, uncontrollable thing that sideswipes us out of nowhere. It's the product of a long process of gestation. It begins with the fertilization of a good desire with a corrupting temptation. It moves to the womb of our mind where we doubt the boundaries of God or of our conscience. We can feel the baby start to kick inside of us. And then sin is born – a bleeding, kicking, screaming act of defiance and rebellion against God.

It may seem that person who "suddenly" has an affair, or "goes postal" at work does it out of nowhere. *"I never thought they were that sort of person,"* the neighbors will tell the reporters. But it's not out of nowhere. Unseen to anyone, deep in their heart and mind, a battle of thought and desire was going on inside of them.

Those who fail to feed their mind with spiritual truth, and shore up their character with godly friends, who neglect the strengthening of their will with smaller, scarcely detectable acts of integrity are being set up for a slaughter.

Long before a bridge "unexpectedly" collapses, soil shifts, moorings erode, and braces weaken, preparing it for disaster.

1. Think of a great sin failure of yours recently. Did it really come out of nowhere? What were some of its roots?

2. Why do you think it is that the further in we go down on the path of temptation, the harder it is to turn back around?

Prayer

My Jesus, for thee all the follies of sin I resign. It's so easy to sing. But in the crucible of daily life, it's often another story. Help me Lord to call to mind early and often what you suffered on the cross for me. You bought my soul with an incalculable price – your holy blood. May that thought matter to me more and more, and compel me to live for you.

The Cycle Of Sin: Death

"For the wages of sin is death, but the free gift of God is eternal life in Christ Jesus our Lord." – Romans 6:23

The hit show *Breaking Bad* follows the descent into depravity of Walter White who evolves from a mild-mannered chemistry teacher into a ruthless drug lord. His motive sounds noble at first glance. Learning that he has advanced cancer, he wants to provide for his family's financial future after his death.

But we quickly see that there are other desires at work in his heart. A desire for control. And vengeance. And for others to pat him on the back and stroke his ego. As initial guilt wears off for the crimes he's committing, he gets good at doing bad, and each and every step downwards he takes is made with a bodyguard of lies and self-deception.

The show ends with the death of Walter White, whose heart is now black as night. But one thing is obvious for the viewers who take the journey with him – long before his body died, death was wreaking havoc all around him. The first to go was his conscience. Then death destroyed his marriage. It brought ruin to his extended family. It murdered countless souls lost in addiction to the drugs he manufactured. It sickened everything and everyone he came in contact with.

According to James, *death* is the final stage in the cycle of sin. The Bible tells us bluntly that the *"wages of sin is death"* (Rom.3:23), but we mustn't be so wooden in our interpretation to see death as what happens at the end of the line. Rather it is a relentless and ruthless companion all along life's road.

God warned Adam and Eve that "the day" they touched of sin, they would die (Gen.2:17), yet Adam and Eve lived for centuries afterwards. But God was right – for the very day they sinned, we see Adam and Eve begin to tear each other apart with blame and accusation. Death passes along to their first children, Cain and Abel, in the form of jealousy, bitterness and murder.

Every bit of sin we leave unattended inside our hearts – pride, lust, fear, envy, resentment – will advance in size and strength like a cancer cell. And death will show itself in short order. *"To enter a sinning state is to enter a declining state,"* warned a wise Puritan writer.

Thankfully, there is a remedy for sin's malignancy. It flowed out from the Cross of Calvary on which Jesus Christ died. *"There is a fountain filled with blood, Drawn from Immanuel's veins, And sinners plunged beneath that flood, Lose all their guilty stains."*

His death puts to death our death, if you can see through the redundancy. His death allows us to be forgiven, and through that forgiveness, something new stirs to life within us.

Jesus becomes a warrior in our hearts to help us resist the spread of sin inside of us. And though we will still die physically at the end of our days, that death will not permanently claim us. *"You will be with me in paradise,"* Jesus promises.

How you experience this for yourself begins with something the Bible calls *repentance.* Which is more than just saying sorry. Repentance is coming to Jesus and falling before him with sorrow in your heart for how you have broken his heart. But it's also rising to your feet with a new determination to grab hold of Jesus, and grant him permission to teach and train you to stop your sinning.

1. "To enter a sinning state is to enter a declining state." How so?

2. Sometimes we look at the wreckage that sin does to other people and we think, "It will be different with me." We pretend that we can dabble with sin, and it won't hurt us. What should we be thinking instead?

Prayer

Forgive me my Lord Jesus for fraternizing with sin. For pretending that I can dabble with it, or keep it like a pet in a cage, to take out at my pleasure. For thinking that while sin has laid waste to others, the outcome will be different with me. Because I'm stronger and smarter. I'll know when to draw back. It is such foolishness to think this way Lord. You call me to pick up my cross and follow you. You call me to count myself dead to sin. You call me to put to death what is earthly in me. I have been crucified with Christ. It is no longer I who live, but Christ who lives in me. Help me to live under the Cross today.

"Blessed are the peacemakers, for they shall be called sons of God."

Peacemaking: Why It's Important

"Blessed are the peacemakers, for they will be called sons of God." –
Matthew 5:9

In 1992 Los Angeles exploded in race riots, after four police officers, who were captured on videotape beating a black man named Rodney King, were acquitted by a jury. In the violence that followed, 58 people lost their lives, 11,000 were arrested, and property damage exceeded $1 billion.

During the storm of rioting, King himself came on TV and asked, "Can we all get along?" His question has sense morphed into an often-repeated cultural meme: *Why can't we all just get along?*

King's plea was not a Pollyanish view that disagreements shouldn't happen in society. We are human, and part of being human is that we each look at the world through different sets of eyes and through different experiences. It's an old joke in Baptist circles: *What do you get when you put two Baptists together? Answer: Three opinions.*

The apostle Paul wrote to the Corinthians: *"I hear that there are divisions among you. And I believe it in part, for there must be factions among you in order that those who are genuine among you may be recognized." (1 Cor.11:18-19).* Disagreement comes with the territory of being human.

All these years later, it could be argued that our nation is more bitterly divided than ever, and that the tinder for another conflagration is very dry, just waiting for a spark to ignite it. One thing is for certain – it is time for followers of Jesus Christ to step up and show our culture that another way is possible. But for this to happen, we must become peacemakers.

But know this. Peacemaking won't happen by accident. The apostle Paul wrote in Romans 14:19 – *"So then let us **pursue** what makes for peace..."* Peacemaking must be *pursued*. The Greek word means *'to aggressively chase down like a hunter pursuing a prized quarry"*.

Pastor Albert Tate leads *Fellowship Monrovia,* a thriving multi-ethnic church beneath the San Gabriel Mountains northeast of Los Angeles. According to Pastor Albert, it's not enough for a follower of Christ to say, "Oh, I'm not a racist." Even if that were true, the goal is not just to cleanse your own heart of racial hatred.

The gospel has not completed its healing work in us until we become *anti-racist* - which occurs when we begin developing a heart for other people, and listening to their stories, so much so that we begin to stand with them and push back at the evil in society that is pushing on them.

If you're in a standing quarrel with someone, it's not enough to passively say, "Well, I'm here with my arms open wide. All they need to do is come to me." To be a peacemaker means that you will go to them. You will initiate. You will reach out. Just as Christ did with us. *"We love because he first loved us,"* John said (1 John 4:19). If Christ hadn't taken the initiative with us, we would still be wandering and lost.

It's been said, *"The first to apologize is the bravest; the first to forgive is the strongest; the first to forget is the happiest."* Our broken world will never be healed until those who bear the name of Christ model these virtues, and take the lead in the making of peace.

1. Are you in conflict with anyone at the moment?

2. If you were to pursue peace *like a hunter chasing a prized quarry,* what might God lead you to do in this situation?

Prayer

Conflict is everywhere I look, dear Lord. Yet in the midst of it, you call me to devote myself to becoming a peacemaker. Just as you pursued me, to bring me home to you, show me how to make peace in the little kingdoms of life in which I operate. As far as it depends on me, help me to live in peace with others.

Peacemaking: What It's Not

"Everyone deals falsely. They have healed the wound of my people lightly, saying, 'Peace, peace,' when there is no peace." – Jeremiah 8:10-11

Living under the Cross comes with the call to be a peacemaker. But this requires that we first understand what it is that God is calling us to. Included in this understanding is knowing what it's not.

First, peacemaking is not compromising your faith.
Peacemaking will involve making compromises, but not this kind of compromise. Jesus while calling us to be peacemakers also said this: *"Do not think that I have come to bring peace to the earth. I have not come to bring peace, but a sword. For I have come to set a man against his father, and a daughter against her mother..." (Matthew 10:34-35).*

Here the Lord is talking about our allegiance to him. He is to be first in our lives, and no one, not even family, should ever take his place. Therefore, if the condition of me maintaining peace is disowning my Lord, then there won't be peace. Not on those terms.

Second, peacemaking is not sweeping conflict under the rug.
Jesus didn't say *blessed are the peacekeepers.* There's a huge difference between peacemaking and peacekeeping.

If you're someone who abhors conflict and does everything in his or her power to never make waves, you're not a peacemaker. You could just be a wimp.

Conflict can actually be a good thing if it leads in the end to greater love and understanding for one another. Through conflict we are given the opportunity to solve problems, to remove irritations, to learn to appreciate others, and to grow in maturity.

On the other hand, ignoring conflict does not get rid of it. It only allows its malignancy to fester, and resentment to grow, while the dysfunction balloons like a lava dome. And when it blows, God help us all. The co-dependent wife who covers up her husband's alcoholism to preserve peace will in time see her home torn apart by it.

Third, peacemaking is not appeasement.
It's not being the doormat and allowing the other person to walk all over you. *"Well, the Bible tells me I have to submit to my husband,"* I've heard women weakly say who are being trampled on by a domineering husband. *No!* Biblical submission is actually an expression of power where I willingly humble myself and set aside my power and privilege, to serve the other.

Allowing someone to steamroll over you in the name of "keeping the peace" obliterates your self-respect, and insures that their selfish behavior will continue on its destructive and demonic path.

1. In a sentence or two, describe what you understand to be the difference between peacemaking and peacekeeping.

2. Why does appeasement or sweeping trouble under the rug not work?

Prayer

Jesus, you are the Prince of Peace. I ask you to calm any storms brewing inside my heart, for I cannot give what I do not have. Forgive me for those times when I have settled for cheap substitutes for peace. Strengthen my heart to make clear and courageous decisions in my life, especially with those I love. Teach me the difference between peacekeeping and peacemaking.

Peacemaking: Its Foundation

"For Christ himself is our peace, who has made us...one and has broken down in his flesh the dividing wall of hostility." – Ephesians 2:14-15

Are you locked in a never-ending conflict with someone in your family or church? As you look about your community, do you see only people who are like you in color or status? If you live under the Cross of Christ, then you are summoned to the work of ending these divisions by being a "peacemaker".

It's important that we understand the *foundation or ground* of peacemaking. If we fail to drink from the spring of biblical peacemaking, we'll soon dry up. The world is filled with social justice advocates who slip into self-righteousness or cynicism or anger or despair because the work becomes too hard or too political.

Ephesians 2 is a classic case study in peacemaking, as the apostle Paul explains to both Jewish and Gentile readers how Christ's death made these two formerly antagonistic communities into one community built around the love and grace of Christ. There are a few things a Christian peacemaker must always remember:

We have a common need.
Paul writes in verse 1, *"And you were dead in the trespasses and sins in which you once walked."* Jew or Gentile, black or white, Asian or Hispanic, male or female – we all share in a common condition – we are desperately lost in sin which has separated us from God our Maker. We are besieged by evil, both outside of us (we follow the "prince of the power of the air", vs.2) and inside of us (we struggle with "passions of our flesh", vs.3). Left in this state, we are "children of wrath", liable for judgment (vs.3).

We receive common grace.

Paul writes in verses 4-5, *"But God, being rich in mercy, because of the great love with which he loved us, even when we were dead in our trespasses, made us alive together with Christ – by grace you have been saved".* God's intent is that in *"coming ages"* he might show *"the immeasurable riches of his grace"* (vs.7), *"for by grace you have saved through faith"* (vs.8).

It's worth noting how frequently the apostles used the phrase, *"Grace and peace to you"* in their personal greetings. The order is not unimportant. In recognizing that I am a recipient of divine grace just like you, I am motivated to pursue peace between us.

We have a common Savior.

Verses 14-16 are powerful. *"For he [Jesus] himself is our peace, who has made us both one and has broken down in his flesh the dividing wall of hostility...that he might create in himself one new man in place of the two, so making peace, and might reconcile us both to God in one body through the cross, thereby killing the hostility." (vss.14-16)*

I guess Paul could have saved ink and scroll by simply writing: *I'm not any better than anyone else. And I need Jesus like everyone else.* Which should bring me round to saying: *Therefore I need everyone else.* Which is what Paul says next.

We should share in a common community.

"So then you are no longer strangers and aliens, but you are fellow citizens with the saints and members of the household of God...In him you also are being built together into a dwelling place for God by the Spirit." (vss.19,22)

What this means is that when we find division in the body of Christ – because of sin or because of skin – we should recoil against it, and do everything in the power that Christ provides to build a bridge of reconciliation to heal the rupture. To fail to have this instinct is to forget, even deny, all that Jesus' death was meant to accomplish.

1. *Common need – Common grace – Common Savior – Common community.* Repeat these four truths several times until you can remember them. Now as you go throughout the day, every time you cross paths with someone different from you, repeat the four truths. At the end of the day, answer question 2.

2. What did you learn by doing this exercise?

Prayer

It's become a cliché my Lord, that Christianity is one beggar trying to help another beggar find bread. But it's absolutely the truth. And seeing Paul's message in Ephesians 2 drives this home to my heart. How dare I ever think of myself as "better than" another human being. Help me this day to see others through the grid of these four truths.

Brouhaha Training: Forbearance

"Walk in a manner worthy of the calling to which you have been called, with all humility and gentleness, with patience, bearing with one another in love." – Ephesians 4:1-2

Now we come to some of the nitty-gritty of peacemaking. What do we do when a brouhaha (don't you just love that word?) breaks out in church life? Or at home? How do we fight fair?

Paul in Romans 12:18 said, *"As far as it depends on you, live at peace with one another."* It sounds good on paper. But in practice, this is hard work.

What really makes it hard is that Scripture teaches that there are multiple paths that we can take when someone hurts us.

One response the Bible teaches is called *forbearance*. Colossians 3:12-13 – *"Put on then, as God's chosen ones, holy and beloved, compassionate hearts, kindness, humility, meekness, and patience, bearing with one another...."*

To bear with another person who has sinned against you means that you *let it go.* You give it over to Jesus. You could throw the penalty flag if you wanted, but you choose to leave it in your pocket. Why might forbearance be the proper response at times when someone sins against you?

For one thing: **Because we're all really good at sinning.** The sheer quantity of stupid, selfish things that we unleash on the world because of our sin nature is immense beyond measure.

Psalm 130:3 says, *"If you, O Lord should count sins, who could stand?"*

If every wrong thing that we do to each other needs to be put on the table for examination, and apologized for, then made right, then forget about it. We'll all lose playing that game.

Here's another reason why forbearance is an important skill to practice: ***Because God forbears us all the time.*** Think about all the times in your life when you did something, said something, thought something that you knew was wrong, and you looked up, expecting the hammer to fall, and instead received...nothing.

Rather than take note of all the sinning others do, take note instead of all the forgiveness God has given you. Forgiveness, grace, mercy – that's what swallows whole the immensity of all our sinning. Peter said, *"Love covers a multitude of sins"* (1 Peter 4:8).

It's not just for their well-being either. It's for your own health and wellness. People who are in the sin-counting business become bitter, miserable souls. Like Jonah sitting on a hill outside of Ninevah, hoping to see judgment fall on the nasty Assyrians. God comes to him and asks, "Are you upset?" And he says, "You bet I'm upset!" Jonah in that moment is not someone worthy of imitation. He's a miserable, crotchety old man.

Forbearance gives the running of the universe back over to God. It lets him fix the people that need to be fixed. We don't have to micromanage that.

1. How is forbearance different from sweeping something under the rug and not dealing with it?

2. Is it true that God has exercised forbearance with you? Explain.

Prayer

The further we go in the business of peacemaking and relationships, the harder it seems, Lord. Intervene? Stay out of it? Speak up? Zip it? All this is why I need to be filled with your Spirit. Thank you for all the forbearance that you have showed me over the years. That as a father shows compassion to his children, so you are compassionate to me. You know my frame. You remember that I am dust.

Brouhaha Training: Dealing With Gray Areas

"The one who states his case first seems right, until the other comes and examines him." – Proverbs 18:17

Here's another suggestion for biblical peacemaking: **Develop the instinct to respect and listen to the person who holds a different opinion than you.** This skill is the foundation for a civil society, which explains why society isn't so civil these days.

The Bible in Romans 14 gives some practical advice in how to deal with gray areas of life. The early church found itself in a transitional period. Many things that believers practiced before Jesus' death and resurrection now were fulfilled, such as all the Old Testament food laws. Food fights were happening in the early church! So Paul wrote chapter 14 to convince them to put down their forks and knives. Here are three truths to remember when you encounter gray areas:

We need to get it into our thick craws that there are such things as gray areas. Paul writes in verse 1, *"As for the one who is weak in faith, welcome him, but not to quarrel over opinions."* Notice what he says – there are things people can hold different opinions about. Not everything is black and white.

I love to cook but hate cleaning. My wife Janis is not into cooking so much but keeps a great house. There have been times when Janis has walked into the kitchen while I've been cooking and screamed out audibly. She sees a disaster before her eyes. I see Michelangelo stepping back from chiseling *David*.

In case you're struggling to come up with examples of gray areas in church life, allow me to give you some: Bible translations, worship styles, end-times theories, Harry Potter, alcohol, roles of men and women, gifts of the Spirit, young earth/old earth, Calvinism vs. Arminianism...

So many battles, and so little time!

Here's a second principle: **You need to respect the relationship that the other person has with God.** Paul says in verse 3, *"Let not the one who eats despise the one who abstains, and let not the one who abstains pass judgment on the one who eats, for God has welcomed him."*

Rather than start the conversation assuming that the other is the spawn of Satan, why not give them the benefit of the doubt and start with the assumption that they're doing their best to integrate their faith and beliefs together. You may learn in time that indeed they do have a 666 on their scalp, but the point is – don't begin with a razor in your hands.

Here's a third principle: **You need to respect the thought that the other person has given to this matter.** In verse 5 Paul writes, *"One person esteems one day as better than another, while another esteems all days alike. Each one should be fully convinced in his own mind."*

Rather than personalize the conversation right off the bat – *You're an idiot! You want to destroy the country!* – here's a better approach. Ask the other person to give the reasons for their opinion. Then listen. See if you can pinpoint their logic. Assume their rationality first. You may learn otherwise, but begin with the idea that this person sitting next to you also bears the image of God, and has some sort of cranial activity going on in their skull.

It's humbling to realize that once we're in heaven (or the new earth, which is it? Let's fight about it!), we'll find out who was right and wrong about all of these matters. The earth will either be very old or very young. Tongues either ceased or didn't. Jesus either wanted women to be pastors or he didn't. Someone's going to get it right, and someone's going to get it wrong.

But the fact is, *we'll all be there* to learn the truth.

I heard it said once, *"Christians need to be narrow in doctrine, but broad in fellowship."* Be narrow in doctrine – know what you believe and be able to Scripturally demonstrate why you believe it. But be broad in fellowship – know how and where to draw lines. Be a good surveyor of the hills around you, and know which are the ones for playing on, and which are the ones for dying on.

1. Which of the three truths that were covered in this reading speak to you the most?

2. Put in your own words the idea of being *narrow in doctrine, but broad in fellowship.*

Prayer

How pleasant it is when brothers and sisters dwell in unity. Lord you prayed for your people that they would be one. But I fear that this prayer of yours has fallen on a lot of deaf ears over the years. As far as it depends on me, help me to strive to live at peace with those around me. As far as it depends on me, help me to be a peacemaker in this world so filled with discord and venom.

Brouhaha Training: To Arms!

"If you bite and devour one another, watch out that you are not consumed by one another." – Galatians 5:15

How do you live in peace with someone when they have sinned against you? There are two paths the Bible points us towards. You can forbear the other. Give them a mulligan. (There are times for doing that.) But there is a time and place when you need to do something and say something about it.

Thankfully Jesus spells out for us very concretely what we're to do when that time comes. His instructions are in Matthew 18:15-17. *"If your brother sins against you, go and tell him his fault, between you and him alone. If he listens to you, you have gained your brother. But if he does not listen, take one or two others along with you...If he refuses to listen to them, tell it to the church. And if he refuses to listen even to the church, let him be to you as a Gentile and a tax collector."*

Note the order here. This is as clear a training manual as Jesus gives us in the art of conflict management. **Step one:** Go to them privately, one on one. **Step two:** If that doesn't work, go to them with one or two others. **Step three:** If that doesn't work, then bring it to the church. Get the leadership involved. Let others in on it.

If I could drill these three steps into each one of you, I would do it. If I could reach through the book or screen right now and shake you, I would do it. (Feel me shaking you?)

Now I get it. There are a couple of things Jesus says here that seem counterintuitive to us. First, he tells *us* to go to them. That doesn't seem right! They're the ones who hurt us. But if we wait for them to come to us, we might stay stuck in our resentment for a long time.

There's a good chance they're completely oblivious to how we're feeling.

The other thing Jesus says here that cuts against the grain of how we usually play it is we're to keep the matter private at first, and only gradually bring other people into it. How many times do we do precisely the opposite? We take our hurt and put it on Facebook, we shout it from the mountaintops, we bring it up in our small group, *"Can I share a prayer need with the group?"*.

I have a rule that's served me well over the years. *Always believe the best of the other person until it's absolutely proven otherwise.* The rule is based on plenty of experience. I can't tell you how many times I've done just the opposite, where during the build-up to the confrontation, I've imagined the worst. Then we finally talk, and realize, "Oops, my bad – they're not quite so much like Vlad the Impaler after all. I feel dumb."

The goal here is what? *To smash them, destroy them, crush them like a bug!* No, it's to gain your brother back. That's what Jesus said. Conflict is poisoning a relationship and we're trying to get the poison out. We're trying to restore peace to a situation where peace has been damaged or lost.

I hope you can see why being a peacemaker is not for the faint of heart. This is hard work. And complicated. Sometimes to heal, you need to wound. Sometimes to repair, you have to demolish. Sometimes to find peace requires doing things that feel the remote opposite of peaceful.

But this is what God does with us. Welcome to living under the Cross.

1. To make sure you have it engraved on your mind, write the three steps of resolving conflict that Jesus commanded:

117

2. *"Love bears all things, believes all things, hopes all things, endures all things." (1 Cor.13:7)*. How does this verse support the idea of 'believing the best of a person until you absolutely know otherwise"?

Prayer
Let the words attributed to Francis of Assisi flow into my heart today:
Lord, make me an instrument of your peace,
Where there is hatred, let me sow love;
Where there is injury, pardon;
Where there is doubt, faith;
Where there is despair, hope;
Where there is darkness, light;
Where there is sadness, joy;

O Divine Master,
Grant that I may not so much seek
To be consoled as to console;
To be understood as to understand;
To be loved as to love.
For it is in giving that we receive;
It is in pardoning that we are pardoned;
And it is in dying that we are born to eternal life.

"Blessed are those who are persecuted for righteousness' sake, for theirs is the kingdom of heaven."

Sharing Our Faith: Be Incarnational

"To the Jews I became as a Jew in order to win the Jews…To the weak I became weak, that I might win the weak. I have become all things to all people, that by all means I might save some." – 1 Cor.9:20,23

In John 4 is a fascinating story about Jesus' interaction with a sin-shattered Samaritan woman at the local watering hole. (Literally. It was the village well. They didn't meet at Methuselah's Tavern). We should meditate long and hard on this story because it gives us insight into how to interact with people who are not from our political, cultural or religious tribe.

As the conversation unfolds, we see Jesus model a variety of habits we should imitate. Here's one: **We should be incarnational, by learning how to enter and understand the world of the one we're talking to.**

God became human in Christ (we call that the "Incarnation") to draw us closer to himself. For us to understand him, he'd have to speak our language. He'd have to walk awhile in our shoes. That's what we see Jesus do when he arrives at the well, and meets our Samaritan woman who's come to draw water in the daily grind of her life. How does he enter her world? He begins the conversation by talking about…water.

He asks her for a drink. Which astonishes her because he's a Jew and she's a Samaritan. These were two groups that detested each other. (Imagine Fox News and CNN times a thousand.) Then Jesus says, *"If you knew who was asking you for this drink, you'd ask him and he'd give you living water."*

By the end of his lengthy conversation with her, Jesus will sing it to her in black and white that he's the Messiah. But notice: he doesn't *begin* that way. He doesn't begin where he is at, but where she is at.

Learning how to walk a mile in the other person's moccasins, as the old saying goes, is a lost art today. Because of how politically toxic our culture has become, few even bother listening to others. They wait to hear buzzwords, so that they can slap on a lapel, and then start attacking.

To a non-Christian, the word "Christian" now means "Republican", "gay basher", or "young earth Neanderthal." Creating thirst for Jesus in the one you're talking to is going to take some real effort today. But to live under the Cross means you will make that effort.

But it was the same for Jesus. The women at the well was also quick to slap labels on other people. She knew all about those Jewish people. She knew what men were like. She had everything figured out. But Jesus patiently poked around, asked probing questions, listened, and gently inserted his point of view at strategic parts of the conversation.

And when it all was said and done, he so captivated her that she ended up bringing people from her tribe to him!

Try being incarnational with others today. Don't force them to enter your world. You enter theirs. Don't expect them to listen to you. You listen first to them. No yelling. No labels. And then with one ear tuned upwards to listen to God, begin to speak, and see where the conversation might go.

1. In the theme verse, Paul says, "To the Jews I became as a Jew". What does he mean? And what would it mean for you to say: "to the blue-stater/red-stater I became a blue-stater/red-stater". "To the white/black person I became a white/black person". "To the LGBT member, I became an LGBT member."

2. Am I a good listener? How could I improve at it?

Prayer

Lord, help me to have your mind within me. You did not count equality with God something to be clung to, but you laid it down and emptied yourself. You who were great beyond measure became human. You, a great king, became a servant. And then you humbled yourself further by becoming obedient even to the point of dying a brutal death on the cross for us. Help me to enter other people's lives in the same incarnational way that you entered the world.

Sharing Our Faith: Be Inclusively Exclusive

"The Lord's servant must not be quarrelsome but kind to everyone, able to teach, patiently enduring evil, correcting his opponents with gentleness. God may perhaps grant them repentance." – 2 Timothy 2:24-25

We live a stone's throw away from a Buddhist meditation center, and it's not unusual on a given day to walk by a group of orange-robed monks in the neighborhood. We also live near Hollywood where it's possible to meet each of the letters in the LGBT community in a single day. Knowing how to interact with people from other cultures and belief-systems is an important skill, especially today.

There are two cheap and easy roads we can take, and one harder way that is modeled by Jesus in John 4 when he strikes up a conversation with a Samaritan woman.

One easy way out is the path of inclusivity, where we say, *"All roads lead to God, and we just need to learn to respect each other's deeply held beliefs. We need to be welcoming and affirming."* This is much too thoughtless. And sometimes dangerous. "Theology flew those planes into the Two Towers," I heard someone once say about 9-11.

Another easy way is to default to rigid exclusivity, where our reflex is to say, *"I'm right, you're wrong; I'm smart you're dumb; I'm in, you're out; I'm saved, you're not"* and leave it at that.

Jesus however practiced a unique blend of *inclusive exclusivity* with the Samaritan woman, where he affirmed her worth and dignity as a human, but not her beliefs or behavior.

This Samaritan woman had great worth in Jesus' eyes, and he proves it just by talking to her, which was doubly outrageous, for in that day and age, Jews didn't speak to Samaritans, and men didn't speak to women. Yet to Jesus, here was a life created in the image of God, worthy of love and respect.

It's even more surprising that he did this because of the immoral life this woman led. She was married five times, and was right then living with a sixth man. Her self-respect must have dangled by the thinnest of threads. Jesus could have launched into a tirade of condemnation and crushed her.

Instead he reached out to her bruised feminine heart with such astounding gentleness. This is what true inclusiveness is – it recognizes the God-given value a person possesses just by being alive, regardless of what they think or how they live.

However, this is where Jesus' definition of inclusiveness differs from the modern idea. Today we are told that to affirm another person's worth we must also affirm their beliefs and behaviors. Otherwise we *hate* them (which is such a bewildering conclusion.)

Well no we don't. As his conversation with the woman continues, Jesus points out to her where her life has gone astray, then offers her a better path to follow. He also points out to her where her religious beliefs are incorrect. *"Salvation is from the Jews,"* he says with a most politically-incorrect frankness.

Any parent knows full-well what this is about, because they do it all the time with their children. Sure, there are times when any parent can empathize with ancient cultures that practiced child sacrifice. (Be honest!) But instead good parents accept and love their child warts and all – which brings them into a relationship with the child. Then because of that relationship, they begin the work of turning their little monster into a responsible, disciplined human being.

There it is – *inclusive exclusivity.* Affirming while not affirming at the same time.

So when you cross paths with the Buddhist monk in his orange robe, or that transgendered person that finds his or her way into your church (sorry, not using the contrived pronouns; *salvation is from the Jews,* and they taught two genders) – remember the goal. Not to win a debate, or awe them with your righteousness, but to win a living, breathing soul which bears the imprint of God's image, and for whom Jesus died.

1. Put it in your own words, in a sentence or two. What does it mean to be inclusively exclusive?

2. When someone says that you *hate* a person for not going along with their beliefs, how would you reply?

Prayer

Jesus, you are so cool! To watch you in action in John 4 with this Samaritan woman leaves me breathless. The way you stood up for God's truth without lambasting her. The way you brought light to her sin-darkened heart without chasing her away. The way you overcame all the stereotypes she must have held about Jews, about men, and about religious people, and kept the conversation going. The way you showed patience, not exasperation. The way you never raised your voice. The way you loved her back to life. If this is what it means to be a 'fisher of men' then show me how to follow your example.

Sharing Our Faith: Be Informed

"Always be prepared to make a defense to anyone who asks you for a reason for the hope that is in you; yet do it with gentleness and respect." – 1 Peter 3:15

Jesus promised to show his followers how to become 'fishers of men'. Clearly one aspect of this is mastering the art of having spiritual conversations with others, and Scripture gives us countless examples of how Jesus did this. Such as in John 4, which describes Jesus' interaction with a Samaritan woman at a well.

Another of the lessons Jesus taught in this story is that **he wants his followers to be informed.**

As his conversation with the woman proceeds, they eventually get round to talking about religion. As a Samaritan, the woman held some antagonistic opinions of the Jews and their practices. As she rambles, Jesus doesn't veer away from speaking truth to her. *"Salvation is from the Jews,"* he says. I can picture Jesus saying the same words to a Muslim woman he would meet at Starbucks, were the story to happen today.

What we're really talking about is something Christians call *apologetics*. This doesn't mean you're sorry for being a Christian, and you just feel terrible about having to tell them about Jesus. An *apologetic* is what lawyers call a "reasoned defense".

Witnessing should never be a matter of shoving truths and Scriptures down a person's throat who doesn't want it. You can't force a person, or yell a person, or terrorize a person into believing what you believe. Truth can never be obtained so cheaply.

Being an informed witness has numerous advantages:

It's something anyone can learn. Apologetics requires you to do some homework. You read a little, think a little, practice a little, and in time, you improve in your ability to have spiritual conversations.

It defuses emotion from the conversation. These days, discussions of conflicting ideas quickly degenerate into yelling matches or Tweet storms. But when you exchange ideas – when you begin to ask the other, "*Why* do you believe that?", something powerful can happen.

It doesn't require you to have all the answers. The Christian worldview is powerfully coherent and compelling. But you'll only learn this as you put your faith "out there", and let it go toe-to-toe with other worldviews. And if you get your butt kicked, that's okay. Read a little more, and think a little more.

For example: Our culture's assault on biblical sexual ethics has forced followers of Christ to dig far deeper into God's plan for human sexuality than any generation of Christians before it. This isn't a bad thing. It's given us far greater compassion for anyone who struggles with sexual identity issues than past generations of Christians ever showed.

But it's also deepened the moorings of our faith. Nowadays, Christians who hold the line against LGBT ideology can do so with greater confidence than past Christians could. Not only can we quote the Scriptures which point to God's boundaries, but we can give reasons for why God set those boundaries in the first place. And why it's not hate which prompts us to point to those boundaries, but it's one of the highest expressions of love imaginable.

1. Give yourself a score with how you think you do with "apologetics".

Absolutely Stink   3   2   1   0   1   2   3   Absolutely Shine

2. What are some practical things you can do to raise your score?

Prayer

Spirit of God, you promised to help me when it comes to sharing my faith. Jesus said I would receive power when the Holy Spirit came on me, and I would be his witness. But Scripture also tells me that I have a work to do. If I'm to be prepared to do this, and do it well, then there are truths to be learned, and skills to master, and books to be read, and classes to take. And most importantly, I must put myself out there and start striking up spiritual conversations with others. Though I'm nervous about this, I trust you Lord to guide me and help me.

"Blessed are you when others revile you and persecute you and utter all kinds of evil against you falsely on my account. Rejoice and be glad, for your reward is great in heaven."

Joy: The Birthright Of The Christian

"You make known to me the path of life; in your presence there is fullness of joy; at your right hand are pleasures forevermore." – Psalm 16:11

What's the last thing you usually hear before a redneck dies? 'Hey y'all – watch this!'

Go ahead. Laugh a little. It's good for you. Did you know that joy and Jesus go hand in hand? You might not know it by walking into many a church, but it's true. Joy is part of the birthright of being a Christian.

Jesus wants his followers to have joy. How do we know that? Well, **first Jesus said so.** Our Lord said in John 15:11 that he taught his disciples *"...that my joy may be in you and that your joy may be full."*

Furthermore, we know God wants you to have joy in your life because **joy is one of the nine fruit of the Spirit which God gives to every believer.** *"But the fruit of the Spirit is love, joy, peace, patience, kindness, goodness, faithfulness, gentleness and self-control."* (Galatians 5:22).

Scientists who study human behavior will say that people's dispositions and moods are largely innate, a product of birth and genetics. Some babies are born happy, some are born grumpy. No doubt, a good deal of who we are is a product of how God wires us.

But the good news of Christianity is that genetics is not our destiny. By the power of Christ in us, we can alter our course, and set sail for new horizons. *"If anyone is in Christ, he is a new creation"* the Bible promises (2 Cor.5:17).

Thirdly, we know that God wants his people to have joy because **joy is at the very heart of God's nature, and we are created in his image.** Zephaniah 3:17 says, *"The Lord your God is with you, he is mighty to save. He will take great delight in you, he will quiet you with his love, he will rejoice over you with singing."*

If you could lock eyes with Jesus right now, what expression do you imagine would be on his face? If many a Christian were to honestly answer that question, they would imagine God frowning at them, or worse, shaking his head in disgust.

But Zephaniah says that God takes great delight in you, and – imagine this! – sings over you. God knows that the infection of sin is in us, and he knows that getting it out is going to be a long, hard struggle. What do you think the Cross of Jesus Christ is all about anyway?

It's God being angry at me, you say.

It's about God being angry at sin, and at Satan, for sure – but not you. It wasn't just God's wrath and anger at sin that sent Jesus to the cross. It was love and joy for you and me.

Hebrews 12:2 says that Jesus *"for the joy set before him, endured the cross, scorning its shame."*

What joy could Jesus possibly feel in the thought of going to the cross? you ask. The joy of you being forgiven, cleansed, made new by his sacrifice, and adopted into God's family, never to be lost again. That joy.

1. "Joy is at the very heart of God's nature." Do you agree with this? Can you imagine Jesus ever smiling? Can you imagine him smiling *at you?*

2. How much joy would you say you have experienced in your life recently? Put a star beside one sentence you read in today's devotional that spoke to your heart.

Prayer

Holy Spirit, Breath of Heaven, joy is one of the fruit you would grow in my life. Your word tells me that the 'joy of the Lord is my strength'. Teach me this week more about joy. Bring me to its fountain and cause me to drink deeply from it. Fill me overflowing with true and living joy, no matter what I am going through. Help me to taste and see that the Lord is good.

Rejoice In the Goodness Of God

"Great is the Lord, and greatly to be praised...The Lord is good to all, and his mercy is over all that he has made." – Psalm 145:3,9

That Christians say God is great shouldn't be so surprising. It's what Christians say next that sends people running for the exits. We also say that God is *good.*

Here is where the need for faith kicks in. To say that God is great seems undeniable looking at this vast creation. But to say God is good can sometimes stick in the throat. Walk on a children's cancer ward and tell me that God is good. Why would God permit hurricanes to ravage an island nation already crushed by poverty? How can a good God allow mad dictators to tyrannize their people?

And yet, think about it. You think we have it bad! King David lived 3,000 years ago. No anesthesia. An average lifespan of less than fifty. No x-rays to find the sore tooth, and no dentists to get the sore tooth out. Get a kidney stone, it would kill you. No ice cream. You had to walk everywhere. Plagues of smallpox were routine. No electricity. Winters came long and hard. No hot showers. You think your underarms smell bad now? The threat of invasion from the Philistine next door or the Assyrian a thousand miles away was always looming. And if those armies didn't come, the locusts always would.

Yet it is a man from *this time and this place* who wrote, *"The Lord is good to all, and his mercy is over all that he has made."*

How could he write these words? Because David held solidly in his heart two core beliefs which we from the 21st century are fuzzy about. The first is that life on this side of heaven will always be what Thomas Hobbes called it: *nasty, short and brutish.* David looked at life on earth and compared it to a vapor, to evening grass, to a morning mist. He accepted this as a hard and fast rule. It couldn't be changed. He didn't blame God for it. It was pointless to rage at the machine, the way we do.

The second core truth flowed from this. God had stooped down into this hellish existence of ours and offered a lifeline to a place where life would last, and life would be blessed. The Old Testament Jews may not have had the clearest idea of what that life would be like (compared to their New Testament descendants). But they knew that when you died, you *"entered your rest"*, and David knew that somehow, someway *"goodness and mercy would follow him"* home, and he would *"dwell in the house of the Lord forever"*.

For David, that was good enough to enable him to call God good.

And just in case anyone thinks that the belief in a sinfree, painfree afterlife is some sort of opiate to deaden the pain of this hellish existence, so that we sit around in a stupor waiting for God to deliver us, David's life rebukes the thought.

Energized by the thought of a good God who would one day usher in a kingdom of goodness, David devoted his short years on earth tirelessly serving that kingdom. *"Trust in the Lord and do good!"* was his mission statement (Psalm 37:3). He spent the first half of his life battling, pushing back at evil. He spent the second half of his life building, doing everything in his power to establish a foothold for God's kingdom of goodness to take hold.

Would that more followers of Christ were as certain of God's goodness as he was, and as determined to not throw away the short time they are given in apathy, despair or indulgence.

1. Too many Christians buy-in to the thought that we get a pain-free, problem-free pass through life, then question God's goodness when something bad happens. What might David say to a person who thinks that way?

2. How might your life be different if you made David's mission statement – "Trust in the Lord and do good" – your own?

Prayer

Looking at David's life, my Lord, I see that the 'goodness of God' isn't just one of your attributes, but it is a call to action. Forgive me for the times I have turned from you when life turned on me. In the world I will have tribulation. That's the deal. But Jesus, you overcame the world, and there is where my hope is found. Help me to begin living this life with the next life more firmly in mind. May I wholeheartedly serve your kingdom of goodness.

Rejoice IN The Lord

"You have put more joy in my heart than they have when their grain and wine abound." – Psalm 4:7

Philippians 4:4-5 is one of the best loved passages of all of Paul's writing, where the apostle tells us where a Christian can get joy.

First he says: *"Rejoice in the Lord always. I will say it again: Rejoice! Let your gentleness be evident to all."*

A person can get joy *in* a lot of things. We can get joy in the coming of spring, especially out here in California where the natives suffer with one or two months where the temperature can barely squeeze its way to 70. Take my word for it - it's *awful.* Sleeping on my new mattress gives me and my back joy. I get joy in being married...most of the time. I get joy in watching my cats. Eating a fresh strawberry. And in going for a run.

Life – when it's firing on all cylinders – is chock full of amazing pleasures, all gifts from God, for you and me to enjoy.

But the thing about life's pleasures that you and I must recognize is that we have to lay them all down. Not one of them lasts. And if you try and put all your happiness eggs in one of these baskets, then your world is going to break apart in the end.

A Christian in a relationship with Jesus Christ is hooked up to a reservoir of joy that will never run dry. That's why Paul urges us to rejoice *in* the Lord. There should always be joy in the heart of a follower of Christ because...

    • *You are saved* – your sins are forgiven, and your name is

written in heaven.
- *You are being saved* – through the power of the Spirit in your life you can unlearn your sinful ways and live differently than before.
- *You will be saved* – entirely, completely, when Christ returns.

Can you imagine what that will be like living in a body that will not sin, will not be attracted to sin, where every thought will be pure, every motive undefiled, every act holy and good. With a body that cannot get sick. Cannot break down. Cannot die. Will never again doubt, or fear, or hate or envy, or weep.

When life is working as it should, it's awesome. Enjoy it. Thank God for the blessing. But your baseball team will not win each year. One day that new car you're driving will sit rusting in a lot, awaiting demolishment. One day the house you're living in and the yard you're tending will belong to somebody else. When that day comes and they put your body in a box in the ground, you'll be somewhere else. You'll be standing before the tribunal of heaven, and the book of life will be opened, and a search will be made to see if your name is written there.

But you don't have to wait till then to know. If you give your life to Christ, you can be sure of it – your name will be found written there. So rejoice *in* the Lord.

1. List 5-7 earthly blessings that bring you joy.

2. Now list 5-7 spiritual blessings that bring you joy.

Prayer

My Father in heaven, I have so much to thank you for. The road of life is paved with blessings that can scarcely be counted. Yet when all is said and done, teach me to place my full weight on the spiritual blessings which are mine in Christ. Earthly blessings give me just a passing glimpse of your goodness, and then are gone. Let me not cling too tightly to them, but cling with all my strength to you.

Rejoice WITH The Lord

"Though the fig tree should not blossom, nor fruit be on the vines, the produce of the olive fail and the fields yield no food, the flock be cut off from the fold, and there be no herd in the stalls, yet I will rejoice in the Lord. I will take joy in the God of my salvation. God, the Lord, is my strength." – Habakkuk 3:17-19

There's a second place where a Christian can find joy according to Philippians 4:4-8 – a Christian can find joy *with* the Lord.

After telling us to rejoice *in* the Lord, Paul writes, *"The Lord is at hand. Do not be anxious about anything, but in everything, by prayer and supplication, with thanksgiving, let your requests be made known to God. And the peace of God, which surpasses all understanding, will guard your hearts and your minds in Christ Jesus."*

The problem with life on this side of heaven is that it seldom unfolds as we would like. Disappointments, heartaches and obstacles abound. The writer and atheist Bertrand Russell said, *"The secret to happiness is to face the fact that the world is horrible, horrible, horrible."*

Pastor Rick Warren put it a little more delicately in his book *The Purpose Driven Life*. *"Life is a series of problems. Either you are in one now, you're just coming out of one, or you're getting ready to go into another one."*

Thanks Rick (he says sullenly). But it's true. And the quicker we make our peace with this, the better off we're going to be. Why is life this way? The downside is that the world is broken by sin and evil. The upside is that Jesus can use all that the world throws at us to make us like himself.

Columnist David Brooks in his great book *The Road To Character* puts it bluntly: *"We were not created to live for happiness. We were created to live for holiness."*

So how do we respond to life's harshness so that we don't grow in bitterness, but grow in holiness? We do it *with the Lord*. *"The Lord is at hand,"* Paul says.

It's because the Lord is near, right by our side, that we develop the habit of talking to him constantly about what's going on in our lives. *"In everything, by prayer and supplication, with thanksgiving, let your requests be made known to God."* Everything means, well *everything*. Take Jesus' hand and do not let go. Keep the conversation of prayer going each and every day.

What this passage promises is not the answer to all your prayers or the fulfillment to all your longings. What it promises is peace in the midst of the storm.

"And the peace of God (so it's not a peace based on circumstances) *which surpasses all understanding* (so it's a peace that doesn't make sense, humanly speaking), *will guard your hearts and your minds in Christ Jesus"* (so it's a peace that will protect us from falling into despair or sin.)

I don't know what God's answer to you will be; it's different for each of us. God is writing a personalized novel with each and every one of us. He's that big.

But one thing I do know – Jesus will be with you as your story is being written, and somehow, someway he'll get you through it, and the story he writes with you will be beautiful in the end. Because he is with you. So rejoice.

1. "We were not created to live for happiness. We were created to live for holiness." What does David Brooks mean?

2. Read the theme verse from Habakkuk again. How in the world can Habakkuk say, "I will rejoice in the Lord"?

Prayer

Teach me Lord in the bitterness of life to say along with Habakkuk, 'I will take joy in the God of my salvation. God, the Lord, is my strength'. Help me to remember that I am continually with you. You hold my right hand. You guide me with your counsel and afterward you will receive me to glory. Whom have I in heaven but you? And there is nothing on earth that I desire besides you. (Psalm 73:23-25)

Rejoice FOR The Lord

"I will walk with integrity of heart within my house; I will not set before my eyes anything that is worthless...A perverse heart shall be far from me; I will know nothing of evil." – Psalm 101:3-4

Philippians 4:4-8 teaches that a follower of Christ is connected to a limitless supply of joy. We can find joy *in* the Lord. *"Rejoice in the Lord always"* (vs.4). We can find joy *with* the Lord. *"The Lord is at hand"* (vs.5). This joy diminishes anxiety, increases gratitude, and secures us with peace (vss.6-7).

Finally, Paul teaches that a follower of Christ can experience joy *for* the Lord. He says in verse 8: *"Finally brothers, whatever is true, whatever is honorable, whatever is just, whatever is pure, whatever is lovely, whatever is commendable – if anything is excellent or praiseworthy – think about such things."*

What do we mean, joy *for* the Lord? Think about it this way: Is joy, in and of itself, a good and godly thing?

Not at all. Joy is just an emotion, pure and simple. Joy is the raw sensation of something giving you pleasure. God gave us bodies and minds wired to feel pleasure, but that's not to say that every pleasure our bodies and minds feel is from God.

There are some people who experience joy when they look at the images of unclothed children. It's real pleasure that they feel. Others experience joy as a drug courses through their veins. It's a real surge of endorphins firing in their brains. There are some people who experience joy when they put the competition out of business, or when they climb the corporate ladder on the top of the heads of someone else.

It depends what the joy is *for* which shows whether it is good and godly or not. If the joy is for something that is consistent with God's goodness and holiness, then that joy will be life-giving. If the joy you feel is for something selfish or evil, then you have a serious problem on your hands. That joy will destroy your life in the end.

"There is a way that seems right to a man, but its end is the way to death" Scripture says (and says it twice, so it has flashing lights around it – Proverbs 14:12, 16:25).

If this is you, the Bible has only one thing to say to you – *Repent!* Recognize the sorry, damnable state of your life and fall at Jesus' feet and beg him to have mercy on you. Beg him to forgive you and wash your sins away. Beg him to give you a new heart and mind that take pleasure in the right things.

What makes becoming a Christian difficult is there's still this old, nasty part of us that's very much alive and kicking, which wants nothing to do with God and takes pleasure in all the wrong things.

But the good news of our faith is that all this can be unlearned. With the Lord's help we can train our minds to *"take captive our thoughts"* (2 Cor.10:5) and focus on what is true, honorable, just, pure and lovely. As the mind of Christ grows within us, we then experience joy *for* the Lord.

1. List some things that you have taken joy in, in the past or maybe presently, which are not of God.

2. What needs to happen for my heart to come into alignment with God's, when it comes to the things that bring me pleasure?

Prayer

May the mind of Christ my Savior live in me from day to day. By his love and power controlling, all I do and say. Make this more than a song, Lord. Make it a living reality in me. Teach me the mental discipline of taking captive harmful thoughts. But more than just saying 'no' to the wrong things, give me grace and joy to say 'yes' to the right things. Help me to store up your word in my heart that I might not sin against you.

About The Author

Bear Clifton is a writer, screenwriter and pastor whose ministry career has taken him on wild swings from inner-city London to rural Minnesota, then Connecticut to Los Angeles. He's been married for more than 30 years to his sweetheart Janis. In the summer of 2016 he stepped down from a 20-year pastorate in New England, and moved to Los Angeles to be near family and devote more time to writing and speaking.

In 2018 he began *Train Yourself Ministry,* dedicated to helping churches and Christians grow in purity training, spiritual disciplines, and cultural apologetics. You can contact him through either of his websites - *trainyourselfministry.com,* or *blclifton.com* - where you can also enjoy his devotionals, blogs, books and podcasts.

Bear's Books (all available through Amazon)

Train Yourself To Be Godly: A 40-Day Journey Toward Sexual Wholeness

Sexual temptation and confusion is laying waste to an entire generation of men and women. This powerful devotional provides a pathway for staying pure in our unholy age.

A Sparrow Could Fall

A country church battles a hate group that targets a black family new to the community. What the pastor and his church fail to realize is that the leader of the hate group is also a leader in the church.
BROKEN IS NOT A DESTINY.

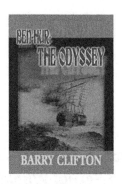

Ben-Hur: The Odyssey

A sequel to the great story by General Lew Wallace and the classic
1959 film!
Thirty years after his conversion at the Cross of Christ, Judah Ben-Hur
agrees to defend his friend the apostle Paul before Emperor Nero. But
Nero's megalomania soon ensnares them in a plot that threatens not
only their lives, but the Roman church and all of Judea.
WHERE THE BOOK OF ACTS ENDS THE ADVENTURE WAS ONLY
BEGINNING.

Made in the USA
Coppell, TX
30 January 2021